Being happy is a choice, so choose to be happy!

Edited by Margaret A. Harrell, margaretharrell.com

ISBN: 979-8-88759-541-2 paperback

ISBN: 979-8-88759-542-9 ebook

Get Your Free Gift!

To say thanks for purchasing this book, I would like to give you this (Self-Assessment) to download for free!

This resource will help you assess where you are right now and the next steps you need to take to find happiness again.

You can get a copy by visiting my landing page:
deliagould.com

I dedicate this book first of all to the Almighty God, who has been with me from the beginning of my life and has been sustaining, protecting, and providing for me. He has been my constant companion through the good times and my bad times too. Without Him I would not be here today.

Secondly to my mom, Patricia Morris, who consistently encouraged me to write a book—giving full support through the whole process.

Last but not least, to Juliana James, better known as "Onel," who stood with me every step of the way as I went through the ordeal of being rejected and put aside by my then-husband. Thank you for being there for me when I needed someone the most.

CONTENTS

FOREWORD

"Courage," "determination," and "resilience" are the three words that come to mind when I think of Delia and her journey in writing, completing, and publishing this book.

I met Delia on what seemed to be a random occasion. She booked a Discovery Call with me, and I soon realized that this lady meant business. She had a story to tell. She had a message of hope for the world and needed guidance and support in getting that story and message out.

I can assure you that you should not take the book you hold lightly. Delia bared her heart and soul. She pushed herself outside her comfort zone to ensure that as you, the reader, journey with her through a not-so-good experience but one that she is now using for good, it empowers you to find happiness after betrayal, divorce, loss, or anything that you allowed to rob you of your happiness, peace, and joy.

I saw Delia grow through the process as I worked with her in my book program and the Speaker Mentorship

Group Program. I saw her heal. I saw her courage rise. I saw her find a more profound sense of happiness, and she wanted to ensure that joy was transmitted to the reader.

Delia takes you on a transparent journey of how her once "perfect life"—a great marriage, thriving business, and financial freedom—turned overnight into a horror story that almost took her physical life because she did not have the tools to deal with her reality.

Her turning point to finding happiness again came after much soul-searching, extending forgiveness to those who hurt her and recognizing that her happiness was not dependent on her civil status and social standing but would come from within.

It is her hope that you learn from her life lessons. That you will be inspired to search for happiness within. That you will not make your happiness dependent on anyone else but rather navigate through unwanted challenges to find happiness on the other side.

Her message to you and the world is that you can find happiness again, regardless of the adverse circumstances you may face. May her work inspire you because You Can Be Happy Again!

Dr. Nadine Collins
Women's Leadership Expert and Empowerment Coach
International Speaker
Author of eight inspirational books,
including The Pursuit of Purpose

PROLOGUE

My eyes squinted in the sunshine streaming in through the open window. It was a lovely summer day—my son at school, my husband at work. I was home alone, absorbed in my daily activities but a little over-whelmed because it was that time of the month.

Not the one that ladies go through. No, it was that time of the month to pay the bills!

I decided to sit down and sort through the bills to see what needed to be paid immediately. I saw right away my husband's phone bill. I had checked the mailbox just a few days before, but I guess he hadn't realized it had come through. I opened it, as I was accustomed to doing because I was the one who paid the bills. But that day was different.

I was not prepared for what I saw staring me in the face, inside the envelope.

To my surprise, there were many calls and texts to a particular number on a daily basis: his first call every morning and the last every night.

I did not have to guess whose it was because I regularly called it myself. My best friend's.

My heart skipped a beat, actually two or three beats. In fact, it was racing. As I examined further, I saw a call made at one a.m. In addition, my eyes glued themselves to the nonstop text messages, up to fifteen a day. I was so shocked I actually counted them over and over again, just to make sure I wasn't mistaken. I questioned myself, wondering: *Why on earth would my husband need to talk to my best friend so frequently?*

As I sat there in the living room—the bill clutched in my hand—emotions tumbled out, fusing into one big ball of everything. I was angry, sad, upset, confused, disappointed, shocked, but most of all I felt betrayed.

What could they be talking about? Were the two people closest to me in the world plotting behind my back, exchanging communications that obviously could not mean anything but an affair? Could that be it?

Truth to tell, for some time I had sensed something was not right about their relationship. I had been suspicious. They acted a little too close for comfort. I dismissed the misgiving. *It must all be just in my mind*, I concluded, reassuring myself nothing was amiss.

Hearing rumors, I disregarded them. *But could these rumors be true? Could these two be having an affair? If so, for how long? Am I really ready to hear the truth? Can I handle the truth?*

So many questions flew through my mind, bunched together, but I did not want to believe it—that my worst fear had just manifested.

My husband, with whom I shared almost nine years of marriage and a five-year-old son—he was the love of my life. We ate together—prayed, slept together—shopped together, even went to doctor visits together; keeping the romance alive by outings to the beach and to beautiful gardens, etc., just the two of us, on weekly date nights.

I still thrilled to wake up beside him every day. I honestly supported him and felt supported by him. Our lives meshed and intertwined so much I truly felt the two of us had figuratively become one.

Even though the sun was shining brightly outside, that day in December 2006, the conditions in my heart gave signs of a tsunami approaching. The earth quaked, and I could see the ninety-foot wave out at sea roaring towards land, ready to destroy everything.

My heavy heart was flooded with sadness, as if torrents of rain poured down on it. It was truly broken; the material things acquired over the years—the big house, vehicles, the business—meant nothing. I felt like I was about to lose my sweetheart, the person I valued and loved the most.

What do I do with what I just saw?

Do I keep this to myself and continue to find out more information? Will I be able to keep it to myself? Or should I confront them?

I reflected quickly that there was no way I was going to be able to keep this to myself, so I had to talk to them about it.

I called Bill, failing to retain my composure.

My voice cracked as my emotions raged inside. It was like I was trying to tame a wild bull.

After recounting in a trembling voice what I'd seen, I asked, "Why is it that you are calling Brooke so often?" He tried to make me believe he was helping her work through problems that were plaguing her but insisted an affair was nonsense, out of the question.

What little comfort these words brought.

Right there in the living room my mind raced back to five months earlier, when I went overseas to Trinidad to study for my Association of Chartered Certified Accountants (ACCA) qualification.

During the months I was there taking courses, my husband and I kept regular but intermittent contact by one of us traveling back and forth, spending a week or two together.

One very rainy day, Brooke had happened to pass through Trinidad. I was excited to see her, thinking here was a great opportunity to surprise my husband with something nice. He loved Subway sandwiches, which we didn't at the time have in St. Vincent, so I sent him his favorite footlong.

By taxi Brooke and I went to buy it. On our way, we were conversing. And out of the blue she said, "Bill really loves you."

I know that was a nice thing to say; however, oddly she said it in a sad voice with her eyes looking downwards. *How strange*, I thought. "And he said the sex between the two of you is great," she continued.

Odder still. *Why would he be talking to her about our sex life?* immediately ran through my mind.

In addition, I thought that as my best friend she would say it in a happier, more enthusiastic tone. But she didn't.

This bothered me.

It made me wonder if she was trying to seduce him and he was not taking her on.

From that moment, in September 2006, I looked at her in a different light.

We bought the sandwich, returned to the airport, and I saw her off.

I brought myself back into the present, December 2006. Now so many things were congesting in my mind. *Brooke and I had become close friends at Bill's suggestion. She and her husband spent so much time with us; the four of us enjoying the companionship as couples.*

Looking back, I realized I had based my happiness on my marriage. I had looked to my spouse to make me happy.

Happiness was always a big part of our relationship. And now, after finding out that he and my best friend were having an affair, I must admit it was a really disastrous feeling. What a struggle it would be to find happiness again.

Eventually, I was able to take stock of my life, focus on the people and things that were most important, and move on.

If you have lost happiness in life because of a broken relationship, betrayal or loss, I invite you to come with me on a journey to find your happiness again.

Are you a woman who has given your all in your marriage or relationship? You were together for several years, investing a lot of time and money to build a life together, maybe even have kids—only to be cheated on and betrayed? Your husband or partner is leaving you for another woman. Perhaps has already left. Having hardly anything to show for it, you have to start life all over again.

Or maybe you are in a relationship and have suspicions that your partner might be having an affair, but you are not sure.

Then come read along. This book is for you.

CHAPTER 1

Humble Beginnings

It doesn't matter where you're from;
it matters only where you want to go.
—Gene Simmons

As I reminisce about my childhood, growing up on the beautiful Caribbean Island of Saint Vincent (aka St. Vincent), I can't help but smile, as the name "Dee" rings in my ears, the nickname given to me by my family and close friends within the small neighbourhood I lived in.

However, my birth name was Delia. Until recently, while researching for my book, I had not the slightest idea what my name meant.

Piqued by curiosity, I embarked on a quest to discover the meaning.

I was very delighted to know that—well known as a name in Germany—"Delia" is associated with "pleasant, of the nobility and noble." What a discovery of the meaning of my name I was rarely called in my childhood.

In the Caribbean, there was no particular interest in the meaning of your name, although we are of African descent, where a name means everything. A few days after the birth of a child in West Africa there is a name ceremony. The selected name often indicates the tribes, culture, and community the family belongs to. In other cultures, sometimes names are passed down, some from the Bible, or are just randomly given. I was told by my mom that one of my godmothers named me.

I am the second of five children by my mother, Patricia Morris, the only child my mom had with my dad, Oneil Delpeche.

My mother is originally from St. Vincent, whilst my father was born in Aruba but grew up in St. Vincent after his parents migrated there when he was seven. He is the fourth of nine children of his mother.

My siblings are Bert, the eldest, followed by Venessa, Shaunette, and Mitchardo. On my father's side I have another sister, Narissa, could be more. I am not sure. Sorry Dad!

According to my mother, I had a normal birth, no complications.

A healthy baby with just three abnormalities to deal with.

An unusually wide nose, a very large navel full of air, and knees that were too close to each other. Due to the closeness of my knees, it was virtually impossible not to notice the X shape they formed when I was standing. The medical term for this is knock knees.

My mother and grandmother, with every good intention, tried to tackle my nose problem early, therefore attempting to reshape my nose like a potter would do when creating his masterpiece of art. They would put coconut oil on their hands or use bare hands, then with the thumb and index finger gently travel down the nose from the bridge, moving the fingers down to the nostrils. They did this for a while, trying to achieve a narrower-shaped nose, but then they just stopped. If you ask me, I think they should have continued a bit longer.

"Your umbilical cord wasn't cut properly at birth, and therefore as a result air was trapped in your navel," Mother said. "I used to use a baby blanket or cloth to wrap around your belly to help flatten it in order to reduce the air in it," she continued.

I have heard of teenage girls and women using a similar method to try and hide the fact that they were pregnant.

My navel rather protruded, so even when I wore clothes, you could see it poking out under my garment.

I was very conscious of this fact; it ensured that I was well covered, especially in the presence of people outside my family circle.

I remember my family members used to tease me about it.

After some years it just went down on its own.

Regarding my knock knees, one was deeper than the other. When I stood up with my knees together, my lower legs would spread out so my feet and ankles were further apart than normal. The twist was so deep that when I was running, people were fearful I would fall down.

I was carried to the beach, where my feet were buried in the sand, and left there for a little while. They were then taken out, and I was put into the sea, where they filled their hands with water and gently splashed it against my feet. This, my mom or my grandmother did whenever we went to the beach.

Also, bush—red bush, blood bush and corilla bush— they boiled in water, using it to gently strike against my legs every day. People who grew up in the Caribbean in my era, will know exactly what I am talking about.

Eventually without any need of surgery, my legs straightened out.

Whether it was these measures that made the difference, I'll never know. However, I am grateful that in their own small way, they took the time to try and rectify the matter.

When I was one year old, while on a weekend visit with my dad, because my mom and dad did not live together, I had a very bad asthma attack, ending up in the hospital. There were no fixed lines or cell phones around, so my dad sent a message through someone to tell my mom I was in the children's ward.

My mom said that whatever medicine I received at the hospital healed me because I never got asthma again.

In school I was very bright, ranking between first and third and receiving many awards. I was also very quiet and reserved. However, in primary school, one unforgettable day the principal summoned me to his office. I had been sitting on a bench, minding my own business, when a boy named Leroy pulled the bench out from under me, and I fell. Getting up, I started to fight him and ended up in the principal's office. This was quite out of character for me; it was the first and last time I got in trouble at school.

I lived on the Caribbean Island of St. Vincent, named by Christopher Columbus (the first European to reach the island) after St. Vincent of Saragossa. It's located about forty-seven miles south of St. Lucia and one hundred-fifty miles west of Barbados, just about forty-six minutes by plane.

It's home to La Soufrière, a volcano reaching 1,234 miles high, with a mile-long crater. Its explosive eruption on April 9, 2021, made it very well known when BBC, Channel 4, World News, and CNN covered the story.

Being tropical, St. Vincent has never experienced snow, but the landscape was transformed as ash fell from the sky like snow. Day turned to night, with very little visibility.

Over 16,000 people evacuated the island; many more were evacuated from their homes.

My Beloved Mama

My cherished grandmother Irma Gould, whom we all affectionately called "Mama," raised me from nine months to twelve years old in Barrouallie, the largest town on the island. The area is famous for "blackfish," commonly called the pilot whale because it appears that a leader pilots the pod. After the meat is dried and salt added, the flesh of the pilot whale turns black; hence, the name "blackfish." Pilot whales are abundant and are not on the endangered-species list.

A delicacy in my community, blackfish can be stewed like beef, dried and cooked like codfish with onions, or the skin fried like crips. The oil abstracted from the skin is drunk as a medicine.

Mama was a petite, quiet lady—whom people called "Mullet." Locally, Mullet refers to someone who cannot stay in one place. Always out and about, she was loved in her community. She had three children—two girls and one boy—with my mother being the first; then my uncle Clifford and my aunt Elister, better known as Cece.

Mama's partner, my grandfather, was a fisherman I never met. In fact, he died when my mom was nine. I was told that he had a boat and fished for blackfish and Parpus.

One day, my grandfather left to go fishing with his crew, but they all died at sea; the boat and their bodies were never found. To this day, nobody knows what happened.

And so, she was left with three children to take care of on her own.

According to Mom, Mama never took another partner while they were growing up; she did not want to introduce anyone new to her children, with the fear he would probably mistreat them.

At the age of twenty, my mom had two of us: Bert and me. When I was nine months old, she left us to find work in the city. Aunt Cece later left three of her kids with Mama as well, going to the Grenadine Island of Mustique to work.

My cousins—Cathy-Ann, Diane, and Rohan, whom we all called "Make it"—also lived with us. As children, after school and on weekends we gathered together in the yard or on the road in front of our house with a few of the neighbors' kids.

The boys played with marbles or made carts, while the girls played hopscotch, dodge, or jacks. We also played card games locally known as Go through Pack and 7, 8, 9, 10 Jack. Sometimes, using plastic bags, sticks from the coconut branch, and thread, we made our own kites. We competed to see whose kite flew the highest.

I loved living with Mama. She had this way of making me feel special; always kind and gentle but very strict when need be.

As children, we hung out at the nearby beach, and many times on weekends Mama walked us there, but she never came in the water. I never asked her why but thought maybe it had something to do with my grandfather, the love of her life, dying at sea.

Mama belonged to the Spiritual Baptist faith, a Christian religion created by enslaved Africans in the plantations they came to in the former British West Indies, predominantly in the islands of Grenada, St. Vincent and the Grenadines (SVG), Tobago, and the Virgin Islands.

Followers very vocally sing, pray, and preach. Due to the practice of invoking the Holy Spirit during worship, they prefer the term "spiritual." I remember going to services and coming back after midnight. Most times the church, being small, was packed. We would be outside, looking through the window or door. I'd watch for when they "caught" the spirit and started making strange sounds and movements with their arms and body.

Depending on the service, buns and juice might be given away free, which we enjoyed.

Although a Spiritual Baptist, Mama sent us to Sunday school at the Anglican church.

For weddings and harvest she liked dressing the three of us girls the same. So, she had dresses made from the same cloth.

On Sunday evenings Mama dressed us up in our Sunday best and took us to soccer matches, harvest time, and other community events, where we bought treats—tarts, coconut slices, coconut sugar cake, fudge and other sweets.

One thing you need to know about Mama, she loved to smoke tobacco every evening unless she ran out. First, she would take the pipe and knock it against a hard surface, then break the tobacco into smaller pieces and push them into the pipe. Then light a match and put it on the tobacco. I could still see the smoke puffs coming out of her mouth, gliding into the air.

Even though she had very little education, Mama was extremely industrious. In fact, she made a living washing other people's clothes by hand. At the time, washing machines were not common.

What was common was that people would gather by the river to wash clothes and bathe. It was almost like a community center since so many people congregated, chatting while they washed and took what looked like luxury baths, as some parts of the river had deep holes that made natural sectioned pools.

When not washing or ironing clothes to earn a living, Mama would go by the seaside to cut up blackfish and Parpus. It could be that it made her feel closer to my grandfather, whom she had lost so many years ago.

Whenever she went to work and was given lunch, instead of eating it by herself, she brought it home, taking that small bowl of food and giving a bite to all five of us.

Every Saturday evening, Mama worked with a lady to bake bread and coconut slices in a stone oven, heated up with wood and closed up with a door. As children, we loved going there because we got to play with other kids and eat the delicious bread and coconut slices.

As Mama was out trying to make a living to look after us, as young as nine years old, I had to manage the home. I helped with the ironing, washing, and cleaning. Also, she would leave money for me to buy groceries and to prepare dinner for us all.

In my little mind, I used to always say that when she died, I would go into the coffin with her.

That is how much I loved her.

The place we called home

We first lived in a one-bedroom mud house made from bamboo strips and plastered with a clay mud with a galvanized roof.

The wallpaper was pages of magazines we stuck to the walls with starch, making the side visible we liked the best. At Christmas time we plastered new magazine pictures over the old one to give the room a fresh look, using nice shots of flowers, houses, cars, or locations.

A modern bedroom is bigger than that house.

It had one bed, and we all slept on it. For it to hold all six of us, we used to put two chairs by the sides of the bed so none of us fell off. Every night we all scrambled to get one of Mama's arms to put under our head to sleep on. A gigantic frown would fall on the faces of the unlucky ones, who would promptly wallow in their tears.

Some of us at times slept on the floor just to get a little more wiggle room.

Another thing we would all fight for as kids was chicken or turkey bone. We loved it.

We ate the meat off our chicken, which was mostly the back, the cheapest option. We would then crush the bone into pieces, sucking out the juices. I also loved the crispy cartilage on the bone.

Mama had hardly any teeth, so she couldn't bite on the bones. Instead, she gave them to us.

Another childhood treat I liked is burn-burn. Anyone growing up in the Caribbean would know what this is. When rice was cooked, sometimes it stuck to the bottom of the pot. I would take the pot and use a spoon to scrape off the rice and eat it.

The loo, or restroom, was located outside. In my country it was known as a latrine (pit latrine) and was usually a small wooden building with a door and a latch on the inside for privacy. The loo, a hole, was typically at least ten feet deep and three feet across. Most times, a toilet seat was constructed around the hole for the person to sit on.

Many times, when I desperately needed to relieve myself, I dashed outside straight there, not even having time to secure the door. With the hole uncovered, I was greeted with the unpleasant sight of human faeces. I made it my business to keep my eyes from wandering in that direction, operating like a robot, looking straight ahead.

Not wanting my bottom to touch the dirty seat, instead of sitting I put my feet on top of the seat and stooped over the hole, being extra careful not to fall in. Newspaper, cloth, or even a twig or thin branch of a bush was our toilet roll.

At night as children, we were all afraid of going out to the toilet. Petrified of what we would meet out there, no one wanted to go alone.

Frogs!

For some reason there were many in that area at night.

From the time we heard the croaking sound we would all start running.

We later moved into a two-bedroom house—nothing fancy—where for years the inner walls (exposed concrete blocks) lacked plaster.

I remember many times we'd be sitting down in the living room, chatting and just watching raindrops dripping from the roof. Or we would feel something wet falling on our head, hand, or other body part.

It would then be a mad dash to the kitchen to get a container, pot, or bucket to put in the leaky spots—at times having to move furniture around to keep them dry.

With the rooms now redecorated, we would then hear a melody of sounds as the water kissed the bottom of the container, pot, or bucket.

The rooms now resembling a minefield, we all carefully manoeuvred around, trying our very best not to tip over the water.

A few times the containers did get tipped over—water flowing on the floor, which we had to then wipe dry to keep anyone from slipping and hurting themself. However, it was a roof over our heads, and we were very grateful for it.

There were some fruit trees around the yard. Right in front of the house was an avocado tree; not a fruit I liked at all because of its texture.

On the left, a big yellow plum tree spread its wings out on every side—sometimes even over the house itself. And we would have to cut the limbs to prevent damage to the roof.

Not too far from the plum tree a huge stone soared over six feet high, with a wide platform on top. Whenever I was sad and wanted to be alone, I climbed up there and tried to deal with what I was facing.

Other times, my brother and cousins would congregate there, chatting and having a good time, being mindful not to fall off but enjoying a better view of the neighborhood.

At the back of the house was a big mango tree—with a big stone right under it, which we climbed on to get into the tree.

I was quite a tomgirl and used to climb all the trees in the yard.

I remember sometimes coming home from school for lunch and having to climb the mango tree or plum tree and pick fruits because there was nothing else to eat. After which I went back to school.

At times because we couldn't afford anything better, I had sugar water (just add sugar to some water and stir) and dry bread (bread with nothing in it) as a meal.

There was a river flowing in the back of our land, which came in very handy because we had no running water in the house. We had lots of fun there, trying to catch craw-fish, skipping from stone to stone and swimming.

It was also our laundromat, where we took our clothes to be washed, mostly by rubbing blue soap against the clothes to get the dirt out. However, sometimes after a heavy downpour we could not wash there because the muddy water would be flowing so fast it might sweep us away.

We could not drink from the river, so to collect drinking water, we made a daily journey to the community tap. With the water in jugs or buckets, we carried them in our hands. If it was very heavy, usually when it was a bucket, we would take a piece of cloth, spin it around our hand with the thumb in the middle, then place it on our head as a buffer. The bucket was then lifted up on top of our head, which sometimes took two of us to do.

It was a balancing act as we walked back home, trying to ensure that the bucket did not fall and wet us all over.

Moving to the city to live with my mom

While bathing one day, Mama felt a lump in her breast. The doctor referred her to the hospital for an operation. When she came out, she showed me the outcome of her visit.

There was now a scar where one of her breasts once was.

It was never reconstructed because that was not a procedure readily available at the time. Even if it had been, I doubt she could have afforded it.

She never told her family exactly what caused the lump. All we knew was there was a lump.

It was at that time my mother decided to take me to live with her in the city. She lived with her boyfriend, now husband, and three of my siblings: two girls and one boy. It was not a change I welcomed because living with Mama for so long, I was extremely close to her. I remember protesting I didn't want to go, but my grandmother just agreed with my mom's decision.

I was eleven years old then, newly attending the Barrouallie Secondary School a couple of months. Now I had to uproot myself.

My mom lived on a hill with a breath-taking view overlooking the city of Kingstown, its harbor, and the cruise-ship parking spot at the dock. It was my favorite feature of where we lived. Many times, I would go sit on the little concrete road next to the mango tree a few feet from the house and admire the spectacular view in front of me. It offered good shade from the raging sun.

One didn't see skyscrapers in the city. In fact, at nearly sixty feet high, the Financial Complex is the tallest building in Kingstown, the only building in St. Vincent that had an elevator. Most of the other buildings were two-stories high.

Before me I could also see the freight boats coming and going, packed with colorful containers. The cruise ships docked with tourists, arriving and departing. Some days the sun shone brilliantly in the clear, blue sky, magically reflecting its light on the sea.

Many times, I found myself getting lost as the horizon glowed with a rainbow of colors as the sun sank slowly in the west.

Psychology research tells us that being physically exposed to sunsets yields a long-lasting satisfaction and stress relief. It is a form of meditation, allowing you to clear your mind of all that is going on in your body and mind. The color and pattern of a sunset is unique, different each time.

On the right, depending on whether it was the dry or rainy season, a mountain range with houses scattered on the landscape changed from green to brown.

The Grenadines islands were located on the left side. These thirty-two smaller islands and cays make up St. Vincent and the Grenadines. Nine are inhabited, including the mainland St. Vincent and the Grenadines islands of Young Island, Bequia, Mustique, Canouan, Union Island, Mayreau, Petit St. Vincent, and Palm Island.

Bequia, the biggest island of the Grenadines, easily visible, was only about five miles away, and on a very clear day I could see Mustique as well.

I will tell you more about the Grenadines islands later.

Located outside, on the left of the house, was a restroom, with a public standpipe just feet away; there, our neighbors also came to get water. It was our only source.

The very narrow yard had a staircase leading inside the house. At the top of the stairs was a platform where we washed dishes and did our laundry. We collected the water from the pipe in buckets or tubs.

As I hung the clean clothes on the line located at the edge of a cliff, I had to be very careful not to fall over. A few times I could feel my foot slipping and sliding down the hill and had to quickly pull myself back before gravity could have its way.

Our deluxe bathroom was a small structure made of galvanized steel and wood on the right side of the house. Our tub was a bucket full of water.

Cane Garden, where we lived, is known as a "rich" community, with large houses and maids. However, our area was the "poor" section.

Public transport did not exist, maybe because most inhabitants had their own vehicle, at least one.

For ours, we used our legs—going everywhere on them: to town, church, school, supermarkets, and the doctor.

Our one-story house, though not very big, had three different apartments, in which we lived more like a family than neighbours.

One neighbor at times gave us a lift into town.

He would call either me or my sister on some mornings to offer breakfast.

We would go and collect it from him and return home.

On one occasion, I went as I'd done before, but something happened that changed our relationship forever.

As he gave me the tea and bread, he reached over and tongue-kissed me. That was definitely not the way I dreamt my first kiss would be.

Here I was with a man who could be my father, violating me. Someone my parents trusted and would have never imagined would do such a thing.

It was one of the most awkward positions I have ever been in. I did not enjoy a moment of it.

My body was as still as a statue. I was in my early teens.

How would you have reacted if you were in my shoes?

Back at our apartment, saying nothing to anyone, I went straight to the bathroom to brush my teeth. For days, my mouth had an unusual taste that I just hated. I brushed my teeth over and over again, trying to get rid of it, but it didn't help.

It took about a week for the vile taste to disappear.

I kept my distance from our neighbor, hardly speaking to him. My behaviour changed. I became quieter and more withdrawn.

He noticed. And one day while my mom, my siblings, and I were traveling in his van, I heard him ask my mom, "Why does Dee hardly talk?"

I can't remember what she answered, but in my mind, I was saying to myself: *He is so "bold face" and has no shame.*

I am happy to say it never happened again.

For years I never told anyone what happened that day.

But one day during a conversation, I told my sister everything. About the kiss and that taste that lingered so long in my mouth. I was already married with my first child. It was imprinted so deeply in my mind that although so many years had passed, it still felt like a fresh wound that never healed.

Although we were poor, I loved school. Every evening, whether or not I had homework, I went outside under that tree and sat on the road to study. I loved to study while nibbling on sliced fruit, such as mango, or some other snack.

While studying late at night, I could hear my mother's voice saying, "Dee, go to bed." After which I would pack up my books and head to bed. Yes, I guess you can say I was a certified bookworm.

In the fifth form (year eleven), I needed to sign up for my O levels and had decided to take nine subjects.

However, that would cost hundreds of dollars, which my mom couldn't afford. With very little education like Mama, she worked as a domestic—cooking, washing, and cleaning.

But that did not stop my mother, who was determined I would do all nine. She knew a lot of people and went around soliciting their help until she was able to raise all the money needed.

I will forever be grateful to her for doing this.

My stepfather, Henry Morris was also very supportive by helping my mom and treated me like one of his own children.

This all laid a good foundation and made me who I am today.

Lessons Learned

1. *Your past does not have to define your future. I had a humble upbringing but did not allow that to be a road-block preventing me from achieving my goals. There are so many rags-to-riches stories.*

2. *Pay close attention to your child. Any sudden change in his or her behaviour, could be an indication of some form of abuse.*

3. *It is always best to get help if having had any type of abuse. These things have a way of influencing us in ways we never expect.*

CHAPTER 2

The Happy Times

You were born to be happy
even if circumstances might have told you otherwise.
You were brought into this world
to experience life's greatest joys and nothing less.
—Unknown

What is happiness, and how do you know if you have ever been truly happy? Does everything have to be going right for you to be happy?

From time immemorial around the world, people have pondered these questions.

Happiness is an emotional state characterized by feelings of joy, satisfaction, contentment, and fulfilment. While happiness has many definitions, it is often described as involving positive emotions and life satisfactions. Happiness can have a number of expressions:

1. **Joy**—a feeling of great pleasure

2. **Excitement**—a happy feeling that involves looking forward to something with great anticipation

3. **Gratitude**—a positive emotion that involves being thankful and appreciative

4. **Pride**—a feeling of satisfaction in something that you have achieved

5. **Optimism**—a positive, upbeat attitude

6. **Contentment**—a sense of satisfaction

I can recall moments in my life when I've experienced each of those forms of happiness. I will share a few with you.

My Graduation Day

All the graduates met in one small room, everyone bringing along their neatly ironed cream-and-brown gowns and our cream hats.

While we laughed and chatted, a nostalgic feeling blew over me. Five years earlier we enrolled in what was now our alma mater, Bethel High School, and these friends had become like my extended family.

I was so keen to learn that I made it my business to sit in the front seat for every class. That way, I didn't miss a thing. One particular boy, Andre, usually sat next to me; this worked out well.

On the other hand, there were others who gravitated to the back.

Luckily, I was well respected by the principal and teachers, who made me a prefect—that is, someone who enforces discipline—and later Head Girl in Form 5 (age sixteen). In that capacity, I was one of those in charge of the prefects.

A private school turned public, ours was very small and had only one of each class; a total of five classrooms. So, we were together from Form 1 right up to Form 5.

We sat in the same room, did projects together, shared lunches and went on school trips. Most of my time with them centered around school and school activities.

However, there was one person I grew very close to—Brenise, my best friend. We were both studious and lived not very far from each other, just about a twenty minutes' walk.

At times if I was not walking home with my cousin Cherry, Brenise and I walked home together, along with my younger sister Shaunette, whom I had to pick up every day from the School for Children with Special Needs. From my school this was just about five minutes' walk.

The walk home took us over thirty minutes.

Sometimes feeling the burn in my legs, I stopped for a moment's relief. At one point in particular I had to do that a lot—Sion Hill. I think the name speaks for itself.

At Brenise's house we would study together, spending hours around her dining table while munching on a snack.

I remember how piercingly it registered as I put on my hat and gown, realising that this was the end of an era in my life. Now we had come to the end of the road.

We were all excited and sad at the same time. After we had spent about thirteen hundred days together, the time had come for us to go our separate ways.

Tear-stained faces milled all around me; I could hear the sniffles and some struggling to control their emotions.

Only a few weeks earlier, we exchanged kind words in each other's yearbooks and on each other's shirts before preparing for our final exams.

As I stood on the podium, delivering the valedictorian speech, my emotions were running wild.

For the past few weeks, I'd spent many hours meticulously going through my speech with a fine-tooth comb, trying to ensure that it was perfect.

I looked around at my colleagues, my teachers, friends, family and strangers staring back at me.

Though emotional, I felt very confident.

In my speech I encouraged my fellow schoolmates to set goals and work hard to achieve them because nothing good in life comes easy.

Our graduation song was the inspirational "Make Us One" by the Grace Thrillers. Even after so many years, surprisingly I remember the name.

We worked very hard to learn it, and I was very excited about the "talking" section, which I did solo.

That day, as I received several awards, including for gaining top marks in five of my nine subjects, my smile was almost as wide as my face.

I went home—my hands heavily weighed down with gifts and one large trophy for Most Outstanding Senior. This was nothing new to me because every year the top students in each subject area from each class were specially invited to receive awards at the graduation ceremony.

Every year I had received multiple awards. At one point even the Most Outstanding Junior.

We also had prom night—the girls all dressed in their beautiful evening gowns and the boys in their suits, looking smart and almost unrecognizable.

I will never forget; I was wearing a long, second-hand, orange lace dress with my heels, but I didn't let it bother me that my mom could not afford to buy me a new dress.

I'd been so focused on my schoolwork I'd had no time for boys.

My date was my uncle Clifford and my sister Venessa.

It was a very lovely evening of eating and chatting and dancing.

Oh yes, I remember the dancing because I danced with Neville, who by the way came with a date. My first dance with a boy. That was something. It was a slow dance and I felt his body pressing against mine.

Sadly, he passed away at a very young age, gone too soon.

By the time we walked home through Kingstown, my feet were killing me—remember, I was in heels. I protested to my uncle and sister—coming to a dead halt. Then I stopped dead still, bent down, and took the heels off. I walked the rest of the way with my shoes in my hand.

What were people we passed thinking about me carrying my shoes? This was a normal sight in the countryside but not something usually seen in the city. No matter, I chose comfort over appearance.

Not very long after that at a restaurant in the city I gave a luncheon speech, invited by the rotary club—only sixteen years old. Truly an honor for me.

Exam result time

As I slept one night, I dreamt that—standing in a line with other young people—I was in the number-four position. This was before receiving my exam results.

We knew the exact date of our fate: in August 1993. The day eludes me now.

Although well prepared, I was very worried about one subject: Mathematics, or Maths, as we called it.

Maths and I started off very good friends—even best friends until I went into Form 5. Then, when we started working on calculus, geometry, factors, complex algebra, statistics, and trigonometry, it was downgraded to just an acquaintance.

I remember every day as the exam date got closer, butterflies fluttered persistently in my stomach.

Sitting in the exam room, I thought it was as if some of the questions were set in another language. There were problems I had never solved.

Accounting had always been one of my favorite subjects, along with Maths, until we fell out.

When asked what I wanted to be when I got older, my answer was always, "an accountant."

The jury was back, and the verdict was in.

With nervous blood running through my veins, I went to my school to collect the results. When I arrived, a number of my schoolmates were already there and had picked up theirs—some smiling, others not so much.

As I stepped into the principal's office, he was sitting at his desk with a ray of sunshine on his face.

He handed me the Caribbean Examination Council (CXC) and General Certificate of Education (GCE from the University of Cambridge) certificates.

My eyes widened as I looked at the papers.

For CXC—four ones, the highest grade possible, in Principles of Accounts, Principles of Business, social studies, and home economics, and a two in geography and in mathematics.

Was that what the fourth position in my dream meant? And fourth in the country in the overall exams as well?

What? I passed mathematics? Great! A pleasant surprise. I never failed any subject, but because there were unfamiliar parts of the paper, I was not sure I would pass it.

Next, I looked at the GCE results. Two B's in history and human and social biology, and a C in English Language.

I was successful in all nine subjects.

My mind flashed back to the first day I entered Form 5, which I was now graduating from. How terrified I was. How anxious.

I paralyzed myself by overthinking and felt completely unprepared.

After all, my O Levels (secondary school) exams were now less than one year away.

From that very day onward, I channeled all of my emotions and started to study for these exams. I vowed to continue studying every day after school.

Now I saw that all my hard work had paid off. This was a very exciting and happy moment for me. Also, for my family. My mom glowed with pride and joy every time someone congratulated her on my success.

To determine their placement in secondary school, students sit for the Common Entrance Examination in the final year of their primary school.

Usually, the talk of the day was about the more prestigious schools, where the top students from the Common Entrance Examination went.

However, there was a new buzz around town—about this girl from Bethel High School who had passed nine subjects. My school got a lot of recognition because that was the best result they had received to that point.

Until then, the results were usually very poor and nobody expected such results from that school.

At my church, the Kingstown Seventh Day Adventist, members were also very happy, and throughout the community people were relaying congratulations, not just to me but to my mom and stepdad too.

I was invited by the government to a special ceremony for all the top O Level students for that year.

My family was there to share in this moment as well.

One day I was approached by a journalist from one of the major national newspapers. "We would like to do an article about you," he said. We set a time and date for the interview. During the interview he asked about my family background. He also asked for a photo of me. Of course, I gave him the best one I had.

Our newspaper only came out on Fridays. I remember that Friday when my article was to be published like it was yesterday.

I normally just pass the newspaper vendors on the street but not that day.

I skipped to the vendor and proudly paid my $1.

It was the first time I would be in the papers.

As I held it in my hand, feeling over the moon, I said to myself: *That's me!*

I then went on to the sixth form at the St. Vincent Grammar School. The first year was known as Lower Six; the second, Upper Six.

In Lower Six I started out with four A Level subjects but was not coping well and ended up dropping two—Sociology and Maths—at the end of that year. I don't know what I was thinking, doing Maths at A Level! The environment there was so much different than in secondary school. The work was much harder, and I had no one to help me.

In 1995 I added three more subjects; two A Levels and one O Level.

The day I met him, Bill

In the first half of 1996, one morning I woke with my heart bubbling up with excitement and with pep in my step. Finally, the day had arrived for me to start my training. I'd been anticipating this day for weeks. My family could not afford to send me to university. So, the next best thing was a job.

I mailed and personally hand-delivered many job applications, but with no success. I had so far accumulated a pile of rejections.

However, today I was about to start a new computer course that would equip me with skills and better place me in a position to get work. The internet was just coming out in our country, and I was going to learn how to operate the computer, how to create websites, type, etc.

It was a once-in-a-lifetime opportunity. I always enjoy learning new skills and couldn't wait to get started.

I had no inclination that I was about to come face to face with my future husband, the love of my life, that very morning.

Determined not to be late, I hustled through the busy city street. When I arrived at the office, I learned that about five of us were doing the training. We were then introduced to the staff. Strangely enough, I knew no one.

In a small, cozy office each person had a little workstation. Some of the staff also shared this space. There was hardly any room to move about in some areas without touching someone else.

As we mingled, we started to get to know each other.

Everyone was quite friendly. That also included Bill, my future husband. In one of our conversations, I found out we were both of the same faith and that he had a girlfriend.

Also, he had recently returned to church, feeling that God was calling him back. However, he found himself reverting to old habits and wanted to leave the relationship so that he could live a proper Christian life. Naturally, I thrilled to this news.

A day spent with Bill

It wasn't long before he invited me to visit his church and to have lunch with his family. I accepted.

There is something I should mention to you about myself. I had a strange mixture of introvert and extrovert tendencies. It was as though I were two completely different people. One time I would be very quiet, hardly saying a word. I could be silent for hours. I just didn't like talking.

A funny story: one day my mom came home from town. "I met Raphael's dad today," she said. Raphael was my teenage crush. "He told me that Raphael wanted to take you out on a date but did not ask you out because he thought you would not talk," she continued.

A sheepish smile crept up on my face. I had always thought he never saw me in that light, but I guess I was wrong.

Many years after I finished school a guy approached me and said, "I liked you in school." I was like, "Really? Why didn't you say anything, then? "You were so quiet" was the response.

But every now and then, almost out of nowhere a boldness would emerge from its cave. I would just go up to a stranger and introduce myself—chatting away like we were old friends, probably leaving them thinking I was a chatterbox.

Very strange, isn't it?

Anyway, the day came for me to visit Bill's church. He gave me directions to where he lived and named some of the buses that traveled to his area.

The journey would take close to an hour. Alone. That morning, up very early, I got myself ready.

I met him at his house, where he introduced me to his parents, a brother, and a cousin. I could see that he had a very good relationship with his family and a healthy attachment to them, which I deeply admired. They laughed and talked and made jokes with each other.

It was a small church with two pews of wooden benches. The floor was tiled, and at the back of the pulpit was a beautiful painting of three angels flying towards earth with scrolls in hand, depicting the three angels' message found in Revelation 14:6–12, about the Last Judgment: "Fear God, and give glory to him; for the hour of his judgment has come."

Bill was very involved in his church, seemingly loved by everyone there. He managed the public address (PA) system and took part in Sabbath School discussions.

Then we had a finger-licking meal with macaroni pie, rice, stew peas, baked chicken, and salad—cooked by his mom.

That afternoon after lunch he took me to his girlfriend's home, a few minutes' walk from his house, and introduced me to her and her family.

Bill and I were only friends at the time, so I was pretty comfortable. We chatted a bit and left to go back to church for the Adventist Youth program, or AY for short. I had a wonderful time.

He later told me how much his parents liked me and made it known to him. They wanted me to come back, and so did he.

On another visit to his home, he called out to me, "Look."

In his hand were some greeting cards, a watch, and other gifts.

"What are those for?" I asked.

"I broke up with my girlfriend, and she gave me all my presents back."

My jaw dropped. He'd told me nothing about his intention. But we were not in any way in a relationship at that point.

I never influenced him or told him what to do. He made his own decision.

But for sure, I really admired him for wanting to make his life right with God.

Sparks started to fly between us

I can hear his laugh now and see those around him laughing as a result. One thing you need to know about Bill was that he had a very big welcoming smile and loved to laugh.

He also was a people person, whom everyone loved being around. Also, he seemed to have a genuinely caring heart and loved helping others in whatever way he could.

It didn't hurt that he was tall, dark, and handsome, just the way I like my men.

We started spending more and more time together. We went out to lunch several times, and he regularly escorted me to the bus station after my training and work.

Sparks started to fly everywhere.

I remember going on long walks with him, and every time he touched me, I felt the "love-flies" going wild in my stomach and weak in the knees.

Have you ever had that overwhelming feeling in your stomach almost like your breath is being taken away when that special someone touches you? That is exactly what I was feeling.

Every time I saw him my face lit up, as my family and friends were not shy about saying. Cupid had caught me, and there was nothing I could do about it.

In one of our "getting to know each other" conversations, Bill asked, "What are you looking for in a man?" I knew exactly what was number one on my list.

"He has to be a committed Christian."

"He has to be ambitious, kind, and have a good relationship with his mother," I added.

I then asked him the same question.

It goes without saying, I made quite clear to him from the start that I had vowed to God not to have sex until I was married. I felt very strongly about it.

He respected my wishes and at no point pressured me. He was a total gentleman.

"I want two kids, hopefully a boy and a girl, at least five years apart," I said.

All through my early years having seen some women struggling on the street with two or more young kids very close in age, I didn't want that for myself.

"After getting married, I want to be alone with my husband for at least two years before the children come."

I knew the importance of having time together alone to adjust and learn how to live with each other.

Why? Once children burst onto the scene, it changes the whole dynamics. The needs as a married couple, to continually grow closer together, move to the back burner—usually for years. Everything now revolves around the baby: feeding baby, changing baby, bathing baby, soothing the crying baby, and purchasing baby stuff.

It now becomes a balancing act, trying to take care of the baby and at the same time nurture your marriage.

I indicated to him that it was my lifelong dream to become an accountant and I was determined to work to make this a reality.

"I admire how focused you are with your training and how nothing seems to distract you," he said encouragingly.

My first relationship

It was a while back that I had a relationship with Sam, who came into my country to study to become a doctor.

We talked about getting married; however, when he returned to his home country, he only wrote me one letter. I remember I kept reading that letter over and over again, just to feel him close to me.

Not hearing from him, I made several attempts to get in touch. I wrote letters—no response—and made several calls; no answer.

It felt as if I had fallen into a cactus and my heart has been punctured a million times over by tiny pins. I had no appetite and was hardly eating. I lost a lot of weight and was very depressed because my heart was broken.

It was so noticeable that one day a lady at church asked, "Why are you losing so much weight?" I stood there in silence, not knowing how to answer.

Sam was the first person I had given my heart to. All to be crushed into countless pieces. To this date, I do not know what became of him. I thought we were going to make a life together, but it was not the case.

Eventually, I realize that I had to forget about him and move on. There was not going to be a happily ever after for me in this case.

Growing up, I always asked God to let my first boyfriend end up being my husband. In my own little naive mind, with no experience with life, love or men, I thought that would be honourable.

Looking back now, I am not sure that was a wise thing to pray for because you learn and grow by your experiences in different relationships. Marrying your first boyfriend might really narrow that down. I now realize that.

Study opportunity

Now back to Bill and the sparks that were flying.

When we first met, I had already applied to the government for a scholarship to study overseas and was waiting to hear the results. When I told Bill, he was not very happy.

He often explained about himself, "I like to touch, not just be in touch." A telling sentence that would have implications in the future.

I was granted the scholarship and was waiting for the agreement from the government.

Despite this our relationship continued to blossom.

However, for some reason I didn't receive the scholarship. Not quite sure what happened there, but at the time I thought maybe it was God's way of letting us stay together. I was praying and asking God for signs as to whether he was the person for me. All the signs I asked for came through.

As things started to become more serious between us, I took him to meet my mother and stepfather. They loved him.

Job opportunity

In June 1996, a few months after I started the computer program, I was offered a job as a Trainee Accountant at Pannell Kerr Forster.

The computer course was not finished as yet, but this was an opportunity I just could not let pass me by. The skills I learnt would be very useful in my new job.

I was so excited. This was exactly what I wanted. How long I had dreamed of becoming an accountant.

Every morning Bill phoned me at work—so consistently that my colleagues started teasing me about it. Things seemed to be working out for team Bill and Me.

But we were both so busy, we struggled to find time to spend with each other. To keep the spark glowing, we decided to set aside Tuesday evenings for a weekly date. On these dates we did things like go to the beach, to Fort Charlotte, or to the Botanical Garden, or take scenic drives or meet for dinner at nice restaurants.

We made a pledge not to schedule anything else at that time—to guard it as our time, special like our feelings for each other.

Because he lived far from the city and the buses stopped running early, on that evening he regularly stayed over with a friend in a neighbouring village.

At the end of our date, we'd go to my home. I asked my mom to show me how to make certain dishes I knew he loved, just so I could prepare them for him. The things you do when you're in love!

Leaving very late at night, he walked alone all the way to where he was staying, in darkness if there was no moonlight.

He became a part of my family, loved by them. And very caring to them. Once he intended to go to a function, but because my mom was sick with a very high temperature and I was not able to be there, he helped take care of her.

My mom remembers how he put a cold rag on her forehead. Whenever it got warm, he'd put it back in the cold water again, then on her head. She was so appreciative of this thoughtful gesture.

His family owned a lot of farmland, and we took drives out to them. It was really nice, being in nature among the banana, dasheen, mango, lemon, orange trees, breathing in the fresh air. We always picked fruits to eat.

I remember we had a special area in the fort we liked to drive to. It was on a slope with one side overlooking the city and harbour and the other side neighbouring villages and factories. We could see the tourists and the ships docked from there. On a sunny day the clear blue sky above, the blue sea below, the lovely flowers around, the peace and quiet made that place very romantic. We would spread a mat and eat and talk and laugh, engrossed in each other, the only two people in the world.

I was truly happy. I can tell anyone I know what it really is to be in love.

The day Bill proposed

"Will you marry me?" was the question being asked of me.

I felt a lightning bolt jolt my heart and flush my face.

I was over the moon. He actually asked.

All eyes glued themselves on me as we stood on the stage at his sister's wedding reception. *How romantic, I thought.* I felt giddy and asked myself, *"Is this really happening?"*

I paused only a moment. "Yes, yes," I exclaimed with every fiber in my body.

As we gazed into each other's eyes, he placed the ring on my finger, grabbed me, and pulled me close to his chest, giving me one of his warm embraces.

There were about two hundred people there, but at that moment we were the only two in the room.

One of the happiest moments of my life!

We had discussed getting married before but only now had just made the first real step on our journey. I was going to marry the love of my life and wanted to spend the rest of my life with him. No doubt about it. No wedding jitters.

I felt so blessed!

Subsequently all of the family got together, his family and mine to help plan the big day.

"We just want a small wedding with close family and friends," Bill announced.

As we started making out the list of guests, both sides were adding names—we have to invite this person and that (don't forget so-and-so from church, from work)—and very soon the list of ten went to twenty, to fifty to over one hundred.

Sooo much to be done.

A lot of our time was now taken up with wedding planning. We were both so excited and enjoying every minute.

However, I think I was even more excited and nervous about the wedding night.

"What would our first night be like? Would it be enjoyable or painful?"

I had no idea. But couldn't wait to find out.

One day Bill said, "Let's practice our kiss for the wedding. I want everything to be perfect. Turn your head this way, put your lips like this, and gently move your tongue this way," he continued.

Wanting everything to be perfect on our big day, I was more than happy to follow his instructions.

I really enjoyed those training sessions.

Our wedding day

The big day finally came. I was up at the crack of dawn. Too excited the night before to allow my upper and lower eyelids to touch. All the bridesmaids and the maid of honour went to the same room to dress, at the home of the seamstress who made the bridesmaid clothes. We will call her Sharon.

I was determined to be at the church on time, unlike so many brides in St. Vincent. Some are over an hour late while everyone including the groom is in the church waiting. *Oh no, not me,* I thought.

That day I did not behave like a bridezilla or feel entitled to be pampered.

In fact, I dressed myself.

I can still remember the shock on Sharon's face when she came into the room and saw my dress on. The beautiful gown was not very complicated—a straight, long, laced white dress, with many pearl-like buttons and a very long detachable train. As a matter of fact, it was my "something borrowed." And I was on a mission to be on time. So, I decided not to wait around.

The funny thing about weddings is that one hundred and one things can go wrong, some of which you have no control over: the car won't start, traffic is unexpectedly heavy, the weather is so bad that guests can't travel, your wedding dress gets damaged, or you lose the ring.

For me it was the ring. I lost Bill's ring.

I have always wanted my husband to wear a wedding band, which I related to Bill.

When he bought my ring, it was a set with his included.

Now, on our wedding day I could not find it anywhere.

I was completely panicked, looking all over.

Searching bags, looking on the floor, under the chair, everywhere.

I even had my sister and the other girls helping.

Time was not on our side, and we had to eventually leave without it.

I had achieved my goal. I was on time, but when I arrived at the church, I could not get out of the car even though Bill was inside with his best man.

Not because I was having cold feet or had changed my mind but because none of the groomsmen had arrived.

My driver drove around a bit, then parked close to the church.

There were so many people at the church, some even outside.

However, we made sure that no one would see me. The windows were up; I wanted it to be a surprise—to make a spectacular entrance when I finally emerged from my temporary hiding place.

It was like music to my ears when I heard, "They are here," which was over a half an hour later.

On that fateful (to me) date of January 11, 1998, we got married at the Kingstown Seventh Day Adventist Church. The building, once owned by the Church of Scotland, has a capacity of over one hundred and has a balcony at the back.

I walked down the aisle, holding onto the arm of my stepfather, as the pianist played "Here Comes the Bride." Everyone was on their feet, looking at me, reflecting the bright smile on my face and taking photos.

I could see Bill standing at the altar, side by side with his best man.

With his neatly cut hair, his brand-new white suit, but most of all a grin of an angel that could infect anyone's heart, he was hands down looking like a million bucks.

The wedding ceremony went smoothly. I was so happy. However, as I stood there at the altar for over an hour, as was customary, my feet were getting tired. Hymns were sung, scriptures read; there was a special song, a sermonette, prayer, and most of all the vows were exchanged. The only relief was when we knelt down to pray.

I did not let that spoil anything.

There was only the official photographer moving about taking photos, but when the pastor said, "You may kiss the bride" there was a sudden influx of people all around us like paparazzi parading around celebrities.

Cameras and phones of all shapes and sizes were now pointed at us. Everyone positioned themselves to capture the once-in-a-lifetime moment. In my culture people kissing in public was an extremely rare sight that happened mostly only at weddings.

Lights were flashing everywhere, but I was very focused on Bill.

This was the moment we practiced for; our lips connected once again, my eyes closed, and sparks flew. It was just magical. I think I nailed it!

I remember coming out of the church with my maid of honour holding my trail behind me.

We were escorted into a fancy red convertible car. One of his friends had graciously offered us her car for the wedding. We all journeyed to the beautiful botanical gardens to take photos. The drivers all tooted their horns as they passed through the city.

I remember hearing this noise many times before and trying to catch a glimpse of the bride, even running behind the vehicle.

Today, I was the one everyone was trying to catch a glimpse of. This was not very difficult to do because the top was off the convertible. The loud commotion caught the attention of many, indicating that someone had just gotten married.

Bill and I walked through the garden, holding hands. It was so romantic. The bridal party and family members all took photos.

There was a particular one I really liked when the bridal party surrounded a pond with lilies and other plants. All being so careful not to fall into the murky water.

When we arrived at the reception, though, it was like a carnival. There were so many people, some strangers to me. When I pointed them out to Bill, he didn't know them either. The food ran out and some guests didn't get any.

But as young as I was (twenty-one), I knew what really mattered was the kind of marriage we had after the wedding day. Bill was twenty-eight, seven years older.

As I sat there in the reception, listening to toasts from well-wishers and jokes by the master of ceremonies, when someone was talking too long, thinking about what was to come I was just saying in my mind; *Hurry up.*

I had no intention of staying there very long or exerting myself. I needed to save some energy for other things. If you know what I mean. The last thing I wanted was to be too tired to even try.

As we journeyed to the hotel the anticipation grew.

In the room, we dropped our bags on the floor and started kissing. I turned around so he could undo the buttons at the back of my dress, then pulled away and said, "I'll be back."

In the bathroom I slipped into the sexy lingerie I'd bought for this special occasion. The night I longed for was finally here. As I opened the door to enter the bedroom, I was nervous and excited at the same time.

A man in waiting, Bill was lying in the bed, fully undressed, with a big welcoming smile. His eyes lit up when he saw me.

I joined him in bed and our passion started running wild; things really heated up.

Although Bill was very gentle with me, my first time was not enjoyable but very uncomfortable; we decided to abort the mission and try again the next day. When we woke up in the morning, we flew to Trinidad and later to Tobago for our honeymoon.

It was time to try again; it was better than the first. The more we did it, the more I began to enjoy myself. Learning each other's bodies and experimenting with different positions was fun, fun, fun!

The "man child"

For the next few years, we adjusted to the usual challenge of living as a couple.

We at first lived with his parents while renovating a one-bedroom apartment for ourselves that was in their yard.

With time, things settled down very happily. In fact, sometimes I felt like I was dreaming and someone needed to pinch me, everything was going so well.

When rain poured almost constantly one weekend, we were stuck at home the whole time. We stayed in bed most of that weekend, and it was when our first child was conceived.

I remember before marriage, I used to wonder, *if sex is so great why were married people not having sex all the time, and why were they still going to work, doing other things? Silly thinking, isn't it?*

After the rain stopped, we had to go back to reality.

Bill was so excited by my pregnancy, and even more when he found out it was a boy. He was fully involved in the whole process, went to the doctor's appointment with me, and took very good care of me.

When he was asked what baby he was having, with great pride and joy he would say, "I am having a man child." He never said a boy; it was always a man child.

I remember even before I went to the hospital, I vowed not to be one of those women who made a lot of noise and screamed out at the top of their lungs. I'd heard stories and seen movies of how women in labor sometimes behaved— acting crazy, calling out for their mothers, and even cursing their husbands or boyfriends, blaming them for their condition. I was determined not to be like that.

In labor, I groaned softly; then every time the pain got stronger, I would groan—louder and louder—but never screamed out. I think I might have damaged my vocal cords because after that ordeal, I couldn't sing as I used to for a very long time.

Bill was there with me in the delivery room, watching everything, holding my hand, comforting me. He told me later that he had a good look at his son's face just after he was born, making sure he followed the nurse to see where she took him. I found that to be so funny; we had a good laugh over it.

Before the birth he kept saying, "I don't want our son to get your nose." At the hospital his first pronouncement when he looked at him was, "He got your nose." My thoughts were: *Well, at least I know without a doubt that he is my child.* Heard so many stories of babies being switched at hospitals. I didn't have to worry about that!

Bill's birthday surprise

Birthdays and anniversary celebrations were very special to us. Both hard working, we believed we should take time to enjoy the fruits of our labor. For us it was not about having a very fat bank account but about enjoying life.

On one of his birthdays, I was pondering what to get Bill. The date fell on a church day, Saturday, so I decided I would have a suit custom-made for him. Wanting it to be a surprise, I secretly bought the material and went to his tailor, who already had his measurements; he took my order, promising not to mention a thing to Bill.

His birthday came, and while he was in the shower, preparing for church, I placed the suit on the bed. It was the first thing he saw when he came out, and his million-dollar smile lit up the room.

I was so happy he loved the surprise. He put it on—a perfect fit. He looked so smart that day. I could see the pep it added in his step.

Our marriage club

Other young couples, including Brooke and her husband, belonged to our church. We were all good friends and went out as married couples together to the beach and restaurants. And had game nights at each other's home. Just trying to add spice to our married lives.

We had great fun and supported each other in any way we could.

I remember once the four wives planned a special night out for our husbands. We took them to dinner and made a big cake with their names on top. Then we surprised them by booking rooms at the hotel. That night was just magical. We laughed and talked late into the night and even challenged our husbands to plan something special for us. Then retired into our own rooms for dessert, if you know what I mean.

The night was like a second honeymoon, and we all woke up on cloud nine.

We were like newlyweds with the sparks still there.

On our way home, driving in three vehicles, we kept beeping our horns just as if after a wedding. As we drove through the villages a number of people came out of their homes, looking to see who was getting married, while we were all laughing away.

The people my mom worked for were very nice and they allowed her to invite us there. The house had a pool, where we all went to eat, drink, and swim. We had so many fun times together and felt like a big happy family. I was not prepared for what happened next.

Lessons Learned

1. *Never tell a man exactly what you are looking for in a man. He might just pretend to be that man. If he is really interested in you, he will take the time to get to learn about you himself. "Every woman's heart has different instructions. They are written through her eyes, in her smile, through her actions and in her tears. She just has to find the right someone who cares enough to read them." —Unknown*

2. *Having your first boyfriend as your last might not be best. It limits your opportunity to learn more about the opposite sex. My advice for young people is to find someone you trust who will be real talking about men and their tricks. I wish I had that growing up.*

3. *Take time to savor the happy moments and enjoy them to the fullest. You never know what is awaiting you around the corner.*

CHAPTER 3

Facing Betrayal

The worst kind of hurt is betrayal,
because it means someone was willing to hurt you
just to make themselves feel better.
—*Unknown*

Betrayal is when someone you trust lies to you, cheats on you, abuses you, or hurts you by putting their own self-interest first. It can cause some of the most devastating feelings of loss a person can experience.

You rightfully expect your relationship to be full of love, support, and acceptance, which is why it is extremely hard to go through a situation where you feel betrayed in it in any way.

The most common, and certainly one of the most hurtful forms of betrayal in a relationship is cheating. Yet, what if you haven't experienced such a problem and still feel betrayed?

Affairs are only one type of betrayal in relationships, and each hurts in its own way. The following behavior by your partner includes some of the most frequent forms of relationship betrayal:

- constantly putting his needs and wants above yours

- cheating on you emotionally

- not standing up for you in front of others

- being dishonest—in other words, lying

- using your insecurities and vulnerabilities against you

- emotionally distancing himself from you.

- constantly pressuring you to change

- complaining about your relationship to someone else

- prioritizing hobbies, work, or other passions above the relationship

- divulging your private information without your consent

- disrespecting or criticizing you in front of others

Betrayals happen for a variety of reasons, but they share a defining characteristic—they can leave serious emotional scars.

From person to person, the initial reaction varies. All of us are different, and we react to unpleasant and hurtful situations in our own unique way. Some individuals will, at first, feel surprised and confused, while others feel immediate anger or sadness.

Being betrayed is hard enough, but in the case of relationships, dealing with betrayal—and overcoming it—can be fraught with particular challenges. There is no set list of rules that will help you get over it faster or better, but here are some tips that might help you deal with betrayal a bit more easily:

- Name and embrace the emotions you're feeling, as understanding how you feel is the first step toward recovery.

- Don't feel the need to explain your feelings to anyone or to rationalize them.

- Resist the potential desire to retaliate.

- Take as much time as you need to come to terms with the new situation. Assess the betrayal and attempt to uncover the possible reasons behind it.

- Try to calmly discuss the betrayal with your partner and listen to his side.

- Take your thoughts and feelings to a retained professional counselor or therapist for help.

- Know that you don't have to stay. If the betrayal is too damaging to you, you can work toward processing what to do, and if you end up deciding to leave, that is a valid decision. Often when children, money, and other factors are involved, it is important to give yourself time to understand what happened and why so you can move on without carrying additional baggage.

Studying abroad

There came a season of great sadness and uncertainty in my life.

It all started when I noticed a change in the relationship dynamics between Bill and my best friend.

Having a family, while working and studying for my ACCA qualification on my own, was proving to be an impossible task. I had to take care of the kids and the home and had a full-time job.

So, what if I went overseas to study? Bill and I discussed it, and he agreed it might simplify matters. Speed everything up. But it required quitting my job, which I did.

My stay in Trinidad was to last for one year. One whole year! The first half of the course was to start in July 2006 and end in December 2006, while the second half ran from January to June 2007.

We agreed not to be away from each other more than two months at a time; he would come down to Trinidad to visit, and I would sometimes return to St. Vincent for visits.

Because Bill regularly came home very late from work, I asked Brooke to help my son with his homework.

I left on July 17, 2006.

We called each other every day and even had devotions on the phone sometimes. By August 24, just over one month later, beaming from ear to ear, I was back for a brief visit. All was so far quiet and lovey dovey in our "nest."

But after I returned to Trinidad, my husband damaged one of his arms, *which was the next step in the chain of catastrophic, otherwise-unlikely events.* Innocently, I asked Brooke to help him out.

It's a blur now, but I started to hear rumors they were spending a lot of time together.

Someone told me by phone that Bill gave her a key to our house, which she hung on her personal keychain, with a bunch of keys.

I was also told that pretty frequently, he was at her home as well.

Initially I would not imagine it to be true.

When I quizzed him about it, he gave an excuse; "I am giving her mother Bible lessons to encourage her to give her life to Christ."

Bible lessons? I muttered to myself. It all seemed too convenient. *Was he just looking for reasons to be around her?* I feared so.

"Why did you give her a key to our house?" I grilled him. "So, she can help our son with his homework and chores because of my damaged hand" was his reply.

This meant that when he came home, instead of me being there, he found her with our son, doing what I normally would.

I can't help but wonder: *Did this confuse him or maybe her?* It was like "playing house." Only, it was my real house in play.

I'd innocently asked Brooke to help. *How ignorant was I?*

I had no idea that she had devious intentions.

Once when I called—*after midnight!*—he answered: he was at her house.

Needless to say, I was not happy at all about that. "What are you doing there at that time of the night?" I asked. He said, "Playing scrabble"—which is my favorite board game.

Bill and I had been together for eight years by then. I felt so sure our love was strong enough to survive the separation. I thought we would be OK. *Did I play down his "need to touch?"* Little did I suspect it would manifest itself in my absence. I was so naïve.

I wish he had come to me and told me if he was struggling with being apart, but he never did.

Readers, be aware and think twice about going away from your partner for any extensive time.

It also concerned me that Brooke, though married, had a husband working overseas for up to eight months at a time. And now I was away studying.

All this troubled me a lot. Naturally, I decided to talk to him about it.

If I have a problem with someone, I will talk to him or her directly. I will not just go around talking to other people behind that person's back. I say exactly how I'm being affected. I've found this to be the most productive.

So, I protested to him about the amount of his time she was consuming. *This is how affairs get started*, I even said.

"How do you know how affairs start?" he asked playfully. "Are you talking from experience?"

I said, "You don't have to experience something to know how it starts. Just look at what goes on around you."

Ironically, the same day I was writing this, scrolling through my social media account, I saw this quotation: "Affairs don't start in bedrooms; they start with conversations."

So true!

When your partner starts sharing intimate feelings and thoughts outside of the relationship, creating a special bond with that person, this is known as emotional cheating which can eventually lead to physical cheating.

Most times it's not planned, but when they start to spend a lot of time together, whether talking on the phone or meeting in person, feelings can develop.

It becomes more fun to be around the other person because with your spouse you have to deal with most of life's responsibilities, struggles, and commitments. This is not the case with this "new love." Sometimes it acts as an escape from the real world, and that's when it gets dangerous.

I told Bill being so close with another woman is like venturing out on the devil's ground.

"God cannot protect you there," I reminded him.

He just said, "We have made a vow to help and support each other while her husband and you are away."

He saw absolutely nothing wrong with it. He even accused me of being jealous.

But I read his actions as telling me their vow was competing with our wedding vows.

I remember reciting this quotation to him: "Only a fool learns from his own mistakes." I always believe in learning from other people's mistakes, trying not to fall in the same trap or circumstance.

He got highly annoyed. "You think you are perfect and don't make mistakes," he said, which certainly was not what I meant.

I knew that with his job, it would be very easy for him to have an affair because he was his own boss, often going into people's homes and offices to work.

He could leave his office at any time and didn't have to account to anyone. So, he had every opportunity to fool around. Plus, I was nowhere nearby.

Looking back, I ask myself: *Should I have just dropped everything and gone back home? Would that have made any difference?*

I guess that is something I will never know.

What would you have done if you were in my situation?

All I want for my birthday is you

My birthday, November 13, was fast approaching. Bill asked me what I wanted. "All I want is to spend it with you," I told him without hesitation, as we had not seen each other for over a month.

He agreed to celebrate with me in Trinidad, and I made all the arrangements. Staying with relatives but wanting to be alone with him, I booked a hotel room and decided we would eat there as well. With great anticipation I waited.

The day came, and I went to pick him up, ready with a big hug and kiss. Holding onto him tightly, I was intent on making up for lost time.

I was ecstatic. I had my birthday wish!

We went straight to the hotel to drop off his luggage. The sky was blue; the sun shone in all its glory; though I was tempted to just curl up in the room with him, the day was too glorious to miss, so I suggested a walk.

With no specific destination in mind, I realized there was a park nearby.

As we strolled, hand in hand, talking and laughing, we spotted a friend of mine from back home—let's call him Joe—sitting in a group of people, talking.

Bill knew him. Also, a while back, he had sent a card and a pen for my birthday through a work mate of mine. However, though Bill assured me he had no problem with it, I noticed he kept mentioning it afterward.

Nothing ever happened between this guy and me. I never had any interest in him. Now we were here in the park, and there he was. As fate would have it, I waved, but he didn't respond. Bill asked, "Why didn't he respond?"

I said, "I don't know," which was the truth, but he made a big issue of it, implying that something was going on between us.

Thinking back on the rumors, I thought: *Maybe he knows what he is doing back home and is trying to make me the guilty one.*

It is amazing sometimes how Satan orchestrates things to appear a certain way though very far from the truth, just to fester confusion and doubt.

Despite this hiccup, we were both able to rise above it and ended up having a wonderful time.

We walked back to the hotel to a carefully catered romantic dinner and enjoyable night.

The time came for him to leave. I went to the airport with him and saw him off.

Returning home from studies

As November and December went by, he was getting more distant from me.

I yearned for that closeness we had always had.

The calls to me fell tremendously from a few times a day to one or no call sometimes.

Even when he called, he sounded cold and uninterested.

I was feeling very unhappy and uneasy, but with exams coming up, I had to try and stay focused.

I did my exams, and it was time to go home.

Exactly one month after my birthday, on December 13, 2006, I was on a plane home. My lady visitor came earlier that day. What bad luck, I thought.

Because of the uncertainty, it was a bittersweet moment for me. *How would things be between us?*

Things started out pretty shaky; in fact, when I arrived at the airport, he stayed in the vehicle and did not even come out. Instead, he sent his nephew to help with my luggage.

Shortly afterward, we made up, although as I was only home on my semester break, I could not help but think about the fact that I had a short stay, then would be once again off to study overseas.

I had a heavy heart even at the thought of returning back to complete my studies.

How do I deal with my finding?

Now back to where I started in the Prologue to this book, at the point of opening Bill's phone bill—during this Christmas break.

You remember all the angst, the devastation that discovery instantly inflicted, the turmoil of questions. After I found so many calls and texts to Brooke in the bill, which happened while I was away studying, the question that plagued me was, *What do I do with this information?*"

You know the saying, "Information is power," but sometimes it can be very difficult to decide how to use it.

I sat on the sofa for a while, pondering my next step.

It was to pound Bill with questions. On my call to him, he said, "Let's talk more about this when I get home tonight."

I waited with my heart in my hands, anxious to hear his explanation. Here is a little more of how that conversation at home afterward ensued.

"I admire the way she dresses, her personality, and enjoy being around her. But I am not having an affair with her."

He tried to reassure me of his love: "I knew Brooke before you, but I chose you."

That did not work because as far as I recalled he said Brooke was in a relationship, with her future husband, when he met her, which made me wonder: *if he had feelings for her since then.*

"It's not wise to go alone and talk to females about their problems and spend extended time with them," I lashed out, repeating what I'd said earlier.

He needed to set boundaries with the opposite sex: limits on how often and how long he spoke to that person.

I made it abundantly clear that all those calls and texts were just too much and as his wife I had reached my limit.

"I am going to talk to Brooke's husband about it because he deserves to know," I said.

"It is not your place to tell him," he fired back.

"If she does not tell him, I will," I threatened.

Next, I called her husband and invited him to have a look at the bill. He didn't seem to think anything was going on and with the bill in hand insisted, "They are just friends." His reaction was that he would talk to his wife and I should talk to my husband.

I was accused by Bill of breaking up the friendship, being looked at as "the bad person," overly jealous.

Here we are, Brooke and I, no longer close, I thought. Instead, we were awkward around each other.

Confidentially, I am the kind of person who can't laugh and talk with someone if there's something wrong between us.

I have to discuss the matter and deal with it first; then and only then will I feel comfortable again in the relationship and be myself.

One thing I am not very good at is pretending.

There was still the prospect of returning to Trinidad in January for FIVE more months to face. I wasn't sure I could do it, not in view of the full extent of the risk it would put the marriage under. But while I was debating the idea, something intervened.

Anniversary celebration time

Our anniversary was approaching, and this year, 2007, I was still on the month-long Christmas break. It was his turn to plan it. The date fell exactly thirty days after my last period, or about a month after I'd returned. A few days before the deadline to return back to my studies.

I knew exactly what it meant when my period didn't come by the thirtieth day.

I was pregnant!

That is what happened the last two pregnancies, one of which was a miscarriage.

At work that day I kept checking to see if my lady visitor would come knocking at my door.

The workday ended. Still nothing. So, I went into the first pharmacy I could find. "Can I have a pregnancy test, please?" I asked.

Back in our business offices, I hurried straight into the bathroom.

My wee trickled onto the stick. I placed it on the toilet bowl. And now for the waiting game: a mere three minutes that felt like an eternity—imagining every move the urine made along the test to see what sign revealed itself. One minute, two minutes, two and a half minutes; finally, the result was in.

A plus sign appeared. I was pregnant!

What do I do now?

I knew my husband was taking me out to dinner that night. So, I decided not to say anything beforehand but to surprise him then.

As we entered the cozy, romantic hotel premises, the all-white buildings were surrounded by palm trees and flowers with a view of the ocean set in the background.

We went to the reception to check in, and there he told me, "We are sleeping here tonight."

"But I have no clothes."

With one of his great big signature smiles he announced, "I have already packed some clothes for you and me."

"And arranged for Mommy to keep our son for the night," he continued.

This was a lot to digest. Time seemed to be slowing down.

I remember feeling very excited and thinking maybe this is exactly what our marriage needed to help turn things around.

We went to our room to deposit our luggage before dinner. When we entered the room, my skin tingled, and as I looked at my arms, I literally saw the goosebumps rising.

One of the first things I noticed was a bunch of roses on the table. He knew I loved roses. I picked them up, smelled them, then jumped on him, hugging and kissing him.

Also, there was a box of chocolate. I love, love chocolate!

We took a tour of the room, and to my surprise there in the bathroom was a big jacuzzi.

"We will be having some fun in there later tonight," I said in a seductive tone—at the same time trying to match it with a very seductive look on my face.

Everything looked all thought out and well executed. I was really impressed.

Little did he know that I had a bit of surprise to give him that night.

It was time for dinner, so we journeyed to the restaurant area, where we were escorted to our seats and handed our menus. Impatiently—sure he would be pleased—I bided my time.

Since finding out, I'd been thinking how best to give the surprise. I had come up with what I thought to be an excellent plan, which it was time to execute.

No better day to give him this news than our nineth wedding anniversary.

Not long after we sat down, he excused himself to go back to the room—for some batteries for the camera.

I thought yes, this is the perfect chance to put my plan into action. As soon as he was out of sight, I called the waiter over.

Earlier, I had neatly wrapped the pregnancy test in gift paper, so I gave it to him with instructions what to do.

"Put it on a covered platter, and during the meal bring it out and place it in front of my husband as though it were part of the meal. Do that on my signal."

Wow, my plan was in full swing.

I ordered grilled fish with rice and salad. He ordered the same, as I remember. With every bite, I was anxiously awaiting the big moment.

We both ordered our favorite drink, virgin pina colada.

For dessert I had cheesecake, another absolute favorite.

The night was progressing well. And the food was a home run. Everything was perfect! It reminded me of the good old days when we just started to date.

After dessert I signaled for the waiter, who then placed the surprise in front of Bill.

There was a glow in his eye.

"Take off the lid," I said to my husband.

When he did, his face was a picture of surprise.

"What is this?"

I wasn't about to tell him; I just said with a big smile on my face, "Open it."

He started to rip the wrapping paper off.

He looked at me, then at the gift.

"It is a pregnancy test," he said with a hint of excitement in his voice.

He saw that it was positive.

Unable to contain my emotions anymore, I blurted out, "We are pregnant!"

His whole face lit up, and he gave me a big hug.

"I wanted to tell you as a surprise," I said, finally able to share the news before I burst.

To be honest, he seemed happy with the news.

We finished our scrumptious dinner. Now back to our room for Part Two. If you know what I mean.

The night was an out-of-this-world experience. I felt I had my husband back, the one I married, the one before things started to fall apart.

He made me feel very special and most of all loved.

Very early the next morning while we were preparing to go to work, his phone rang.

Don't guess.

Bill was in the shower, so I picked up.

"Hello," I answered.

"Hello," the person echoed.

My heart sank, and my whole demeanour took a deep dip.

It was Brooke.

With an obviously unpleasant look—of course, I was upset—I passed the phone to him in the shower.

After he finished speaking to her, I expressed my displeasure and asked, "Why is she calling you so early?"

"She just wanted to find out how things went last night," he said.

"Don't make anything of it and spoil the wonderful time we had together," he pleaded.

What business was it of hers? As a woman, I knew this could not be just friendship. They say women have a sixth sense when it comes to relationships.

Too many signs were there.

I felt as though she was taking away from my special time with my husband, not letting me have him to myself. It's like she couldn't wait to call him and was just counting the minutes before daybreak. I wondered if she got any sleep that night. That weekend after church I was telling my girlfriends all about how much fun our anniversary celebration was: the surprise sleepover, the flowers, the chocolate, and the jacuzzi.

Brooke was sitting there; she and I still talked to each other at that point—at least politely if not intimately. My other friends showed great excitement, soaking up the entire account.

However, Brooke, on the other hand, just sat there quietly, disinterested apparently.

This, I found to be strange, just like the moment in the taxi sometime before. *Was she jealous? Did she think my hold on Bill was too strong and it bothered her?*

She made me more suspicious.

Of course, I mentioned it to my husband, who just brushed it off and said, "I don't know why she was reacting that way."

I made an appointment to see a gynecologist, who after doing an ultra-sound concluded that the pregnancy was high risk, and we might lose the baby.

So, after a mentally draining tug of war between returning to study or staying home, I finally decided not to go back until after the birth.

It was a liberating feeling. Reflecting back on the past month, my thoughts had been consumed with making this decision. Not working, most times I was at home in solitude, agonizing over what to do. By choosing not to tell anyone, I was trying to deal with the situation on my own. I can't count the number of times I made a decision, then shortly afterwards reversed it. All this now came to an end.

Bill, on the other hand, accused me of only wanting to stay around to spy on them.

If I were to be honest, it did play a role in my decision. I was dreading what would happen if I once more, left him alone again with Brooke.

The truth is, I just couldn't bring myself to be away from home when my marriage seemed to be crumbling.

Nevertheless, to try and make peace, I had gotten it in my mind to apologize.

Feeling rejected by Brooke

Feeling terrible about the whole thing, I called Brooke and told her I wanted to apologize. She offered to pass by after work.

I explained my plan to my husband, who seemed very pleased.

When I spoke to one of our pastors, however, he was shocked and asked, "Why are you going to apologize to this woman? She is the one who needs to apologize to you."

Tap, tap, tap. I heard a knock on the door.

As I walked towards the door my heart raced in my chest. I slowly turned the knob.

Looking at me with expectant eyes, Brooke was standing there.

As I invited her in and we sat down in the dining room, I was still unsure how to proceed.

But my emotions took over. I blurted out: "I am not comfortable with the closeness between you and my husband."

Her body language reflecting uneasiness like her voice, she held to her story: "I thought you were going to apologize; there is nothing going on between Bill and me. We are just friends. I have never lost a friend before, and I am not going to give up on our friendship," she continued—such passion in her voice.

It was quite clear to me that their friendship meant a lot more to her, as she was virtually assuring the loss of ours.

My onetime best friend made her choice as to who she valued most, and it was not me.

But wait a minute. *Did she even consider me a friend?* I longed to hear these words from her, "I don't want to lose your friendship."

Neither seemed to have given a thought as to the impact their relationship had on me. I could not, for the life of me, understand why they both saw nothing wrong with their relationship.

How could she not see sadness in my face, my words, and my body language? Or feel my pain as I tried to express what her relationship with my husband was doing to me and our marriage. This left a very bad taste in my mouth.

As we sat around the table, I learned one of the worst lessons anyone ever could.

"Your best friend can become your worst enemy."

The tension in the room was so thick that if you had a knife, you could have cut it. This was full-blown cat fighting. She was angry and so was I.

The more she talked, the more I realized that, *No way am I going to apologize to her.*

She left and we were pushed even further apart, as she felt tricked, deprived of the expected apology.

That night, Bill was very upset with me. "Why didn't you apologize to Brooke like you said you would?" Brooke definitely called him and told him what happened.

Needless to say, the distance between Brooke and me grew bigger and bigger. *No longer did I see her as my friend.*

This was the same woman I used to phone almost daily and talk with about everything and anything: our problems, our dreams, likes, and dislikes.

Whenever her husband's birthday or their anniversary was approaching, she would ask for suggestions because she knew I was creative.

Whenever she needed my help, I was there, and I could depend on her in the same way.

High-Risk pregnancy and birth of our second son

Due to the complications of the pregnancy, we decided that I'd stay home not just from Trinidad but from working any job for a year with the baby.

Fearful of losing the baby I mostly stayed at home taking lots of rest and trying to be as careful as possible not to exert myself or lift heavy items. We also decided because the previous pregnancy ended in a miscarriage, not to tell anyone until I was three months' pregnant. However, all that changed one night when we went out for pizza with Brooke, her husband, and two other couples. The seaside restaurant sat on a slope leading down to a little wharf a few feet below.

After eating, we relaxed at the wharf, chilling out a bit.

However, I began to feel really nauseated, as if I wanted to vomit, but tried not to let it show. I hadn't reach three months yet.

In no time, however, I felt like a force just grabbed me, took me to the edge of the wharf, and it all just started to pour out of me into the water.

It was like I had no control over my body anymore.

I just couldn't hold it back.

That went on for a while, with everyone just watching the scene.

Well, the secret was out now. Instantly, they suspected correctly, and we had no choice but to break the news there and then.

"We are pregnant," Bill shouted.

They were the first to know.

While we traveled back home in the vehicle that night, Bill was driving, I was sitting next to him, and Brooke and her husband were in the back.

We started talking about the pregnancy.

"I am very happy for you guys," Brooke's husband said in an excited, supportive voice. Obviously, he was quite genuine about it.

Hardly uttering a word, Brooke showed no such excitement.

I remember thinking to myself: *Maybe she wishes she were carrying Bill's child.* An ironic statement, as I found out later.

As time went by, Bill's initial excitement at having a baby faded before my eyes. His interest way below average, he hardly talked about the baby to me or anyone else. Not touching my belly and talking to the baby, as he did so many times with my first pregnancy.

He was even questioning me, "How did you get pregnant so quickly after coming home?"

Clearly, he was very detached, so I outright asked him, "Do you want the baby?"

"Yes, I am excited," he said in words—his actions communicating something else.

Not only was his behaviour this time different, but how could I forget that he almost missed the birth?

When he arrived, he was not fully there, I could see. His body was there, but the comforting words and touch given by a spouse while his wife is going through such an ordeal were just non-existent.

In all of my pain and the pushing, I could faintly hear one of the nurses telling Bill to "rub her back." Then is when I felt his touch.

Brooke became his secretary at our business

Now a new development. Brooke lost her job, but I found it strange she would be fired just about two months before the planned closure of the company she worked for.

When I asked her why she was fired, she just said, "My boss never liked me."

To me, something didn't add up. I thought it must have been something very extreme that happened. It just didn't make sense.

She took a long time to get a new job. Bill approached me and asked about her working as his secretary. I called her husband to find out how he felt. "I have no problem with it," the poor, trusting guy said.

We both interviewed her, and she soon started work at our business as the secretary.

Before agreeing, though, I said, "This must be kept professional."

They both assured me nothing was happening between them and that they would keep their relationship strictly professional.

Everything was in place, and she was to start the following Monday.

Not until years later did one of her former co-workers explain to me what had happened at her previous job. I can't tell you exactly what I heard, but it involved her being found naked in the office by her boss with Bill's vehicle parked outside.

Now that made more sense to me. If I had known this before, no way would I have agreed for her to work at our business.

Started to investigate my suspicions of Bill and Brooke

All this time, with everything that was happening, I had made it my business to be more observant around Bill and Brooke. I kept my eyes and ears wide open.

Doing this did make me realize a number of things. These happened over a few years and are not in any particular order.

For one, they were chatting a lot online. One night he was on the computer in the study. I went to ask him to come to bed, it was very late. He had closed the chat, but while I was standing next to him, a message popped up at the bottom of the screen. It said, "Sweet dreams."

Can you guess who it was from?

Brooke.

The Columbo in me came out, and I started to dig even deeper.

I have never been technologically minded. I always told people, "My husband is the techie, not me."

I waited until the next day when he was at work, went on the computer, and somehow, I figured out how to pull up the online chat history.

Don't ask me how I did it. I can't remember.

Able to read one of their conversations, I saw that in it she told him to send something to "our email address." I was like, *"Our email address"? Did they have a special one just for them?*

Wow!

I printed the conversation, waited until he got home, and showed him.

"What did she mean?" I asked.

"It must have been a typo because we don't have any special email address," he replied in a calm voice, brushing the question off.

I often told him something I've always believed from the bottom of my heart: that God said, "Whatever is in the darkness must come to light."

I used to pray and ask God to reveal the truth to me.

Later, typing on his laptop, I saw that he had a new email address I didn't know about.

I asked him, "Why didn't you tell me about this email address?"

"It's nothing," he replied.

He raised his voice: "You are invading my privacy."

Obviously, he didn't like the truth coming out that he had lied to me. I felt crushed.

One day Bill and I were standing in the living room, talking, when his phone rang.

"Hello"—he picked up. "Hi, Brooke"—he brazenly headed into our bedroom, shutting me out.

I followed behind him but stopped in my tracks when I saw what he did next. *Am I seeing right?*

What caught my attention the most was the way in which he lay down on the bed, chatting away with her.

It was in a slanted, playful manner.

As I stood there, I could not help but feel like the third wheel in this relationship.

It was as if I were not even there.

I remember one day Brooke came by for a visit. For some reason which now evades me, we ended up in my bedroom. "It's been a long time since I've been in here," I heard her say.

I wondered to myself: *Is she aware of what she is saying to me, and what does she mean by it?* When I was around, she hardly ever came into our bedroom; most times we were either in the living room or the study.

All these months I had been trying to doubt myself, reassuring myself: *Maybe nothing is going on with them.* But her words just brought my suspicions to life again.

Later I found out she used to be in our bedroom when I was away studying.

Bill approached me one day and said, "Brooke's washing machine is not working so she asked to come and use ours."

On one occasion when she came over, Bill and I were upstairs. He went down, unaware I was coming down right behind him. When he reached the bottom of the stairs, she passed at the same time, heading towards the laundry section.

My heart shivered at the scene that unraveled right before my eyes.

They both stretched out their arms, gently touching hands for a moment. Then she continued on her way; they were so immersed in each other's eyes that I seemed in that instant invisible to them, though only a few feet away.

Facing his back, I could not see his face, but on her face, she wore a big smile.

My husband was the kind of man who was very physical, hugged a lot and pinched his friends' jaws. But never before had I seen him touching another woman's hand the way he did with Brooke.

This multiplied my suspicions.

I told Bill what I witnessed, but he had very little to say about the matter.

"I don't feel comfortable having her come to our house anymore," I said. "You need to tell her she cannot come back here to do laundry," I continued.

By this time, she and I were growing apart.

She never came back.

Time for counseling

Brooke no longer seemed happy around her husband, and Bill was growing more distant from me. However, when the two of them were together, they talked and laughed.

I felt heartbroken. Losing my husband before my eyes, I still loved him very much. It was all so hard to bear. I felt helpless.

We had been married nine years, had two sons, and I remember, before all the drama started, hearing him telling his friends many times how happy he was.

We did everything together, very much a part of each other's lives, and always communicated with each other throughout the day. I remember his boss was so surprised at to how closely connected we were. The two of us were a good team, but now—?

What do you do as a wife when you see your husband's affection moving towards another woman?

I suggested seeing a counselor, who gave us a book, *Building Hedges around your Marriage*, which we started reading together. It contained practical advice—measures to put in place to protect your marriage, which included not getting too close to someone else of the opposite sex.

Sad to say, I ended up finishing it by myself; he did not like the advice in it.

As time went on, things didn't improve.

The counseling had no effect, nor did any of my efforts to make things right. Hard to believe, but this state of things went on for a couple of years.

The funny thing is, we were fine, even then, until Brooke's name was mentioned. She became a thorn in my flesh that didn't seem to want to go away.

Somehow, we were always able to make up and hold the marriage together, *but how long could we keep this up?*

Far from being solved, the problem kept being swept under the carpet. A disaster just waiting to happen.

Bill and Brooke working together

The fact that they were working together didn't help the situation. I met them having lunch together on several occasions, and when I asked why, he would just casually ask, "What's wrong with friends having lunch?"

My response was, "Why of all the employees is she the only one I see you having lunch with?" He didn't have much to say about it.

Sometimes when I dropped by at lunchtime, what would I see? Two lunch boxes on the cabinet. She bought their lunches and waited for him to come back to the office after an outside job for them to eat together. What a heart-rending sight.

I decided to tell her exactly how I felt—about everything. How uncomfortable their relationship made me. It was indiscreet.

Once again, she denied being lovers, but took things even further: "It seems like you want it to be true that your husband is cheating," she said in attack mode.

Stepping back in sheer shock, I questioned, "Why on earth would I be wishing for my husband to cheat on me?"

I was very happy in my marriage before all this happened.

I am the kind of person who feels content with what is mine. Bill was mine, and I never wanted or desired another man.

The only reason it hurt so much was that I really loved my husband and didn't want my marriage to end. *I was trying desperately to not let that happen.*

I didn't really blame her. I blamed him the most because he made a vow to me, "till death do us part." In my mind, I thought it was his obligation to break things off.

If he really loved me, it should not be too hard to choose me.

Working in our office gave her the opportunity to see how much money the business was making, which I think made her hold on even tighter to Bill.

I once saw this quotation: *"The saddest thing about betrayal is that it never comes from your enemies. It comes from friends and loved ones!"*

—*Unknown*

This is so true.

Feeling replaced by Brooke

For years, Bill and Brooke kept saying they were just friends.

Sometimes I thought maybe I was wrong. *Maybe they are just friends.* It was confusing sometimes because I seemed to be the only one who had a problem.

Maybe I'm seeing what's not there.

I saw one close personality trait in both of them; they were people-persons.

For Bill, Brooke could do no wrong. He defended her in everything. Whenever her name was mentioned, his whole attitude changed and he became defensive.

At one point, in her defence he said, "Brooke was the one who helped to plan our last anniversary night together."

Needless to say, that brought no comfort to me, just more questions. *Why is he having her plan our anniversary celebration?*

I could feel the smoke coming out my ears.

He started doing things with her that we would have normally done together. When I asked how come, he said that I was busy and she had more time.

Bill's grandmother was sick for a while, and sadly one day she died.

"Can I help with the funeral programs?" I asked Bill. Programs show the order of the service and are given out at the funeral.

"I thought you would not have any time because of work. So, I asked Brooke to help with the funeral arrangements," Bill said.

His two brothers got married in close succession, and together they planned everything. They were the best man and maid of honour.

I remember at one of the weddings, while sitting in the church with the kids, I looked out the window on my left, and who did I see, walking side by side, chatting and laughing away?

You guessed it. Bill and Brooke.

After that same wedding he came home and showed me the pictures. In one, they were standing on opposite sides of a flower, gazing into each other's eyes. Whether that was deliberate or not, that look said it all.

Any fool could have seen the attraction jumping out of the photo. I kept all this to myself, saying nothing to him about it.

I remember he traveled overseas, and when he returned, while unpacking his suitcase, he showed me a perfume he bought for Brooke.

The name of it was the same as Brooke's nickname.

He then told me, "When I saw this perfume, I didn't even think about how much it cost. I just picked it up."

Was he really conscious that he was talking to me, his wife, and how I would feel hearing that?

Have you ever felt like you were being replaced right before your very eyes? Like someone was taking over your job, or in my case someone taking over your husband?

I noticed that she was getting closer not only to Bill but also to his family. They were inviting her to their outings.

Watching everything unfolding, just one of his siblings expressed sorrow to me. Nobody else in his family reached out.

One time, however, I was speaking to one of his siblings, who was saying how Brooke was helping to organize an appointment on her behalf. My remark: "So you have a new sister-in-law?"

"New, till now?" was the reply with a question.

In other words, I was being told Brooke had already a long time ago been accepted. A "done deal."

Did someone just slap me across my face? That's what it felt like.

From then on, I had to accept the fact that Brooke had taken my place in their family.

With everything I was facing, many times, the sadness wrapped itself and engulfed me like a blanket, and there was no glimpse of light to be seen. I often wondered: *Will I ever be happy again?*

Lessons Learned

1. *One of the things I would advise young women is to make sure, if possible, they complete their studies before starting a family. It is very hard juggling a husband, children, taking care of a home and a full-time job while pursuing your studies. It becomes even more challenging if you have to leave your family behind to go away to study. That gives other women the opportunity to cause havoc in your relationship. This is not to say that your*

relationship would be safe if you stayed. If a man really wants to cheat, he will do it whether you are one mile or a thousand miles away.

2. As a woman, be careful with girlfriends around your husband. Try to avoid   asking them to help your husband with anything; get his mother or sister, etc.

3. Be very careful whom you invite into your home, especially among your female friends. The sad thing is, when some of them come and see what you have, they then begin to want it for themselves and would go at any length to get it.

4. Don't share everything with your spouse. It's not that you are hiding things from him, but some men just cannot handle certain information, especially when it comes to other men, and have the tendency to jump to all sorts of wrong conclusions. As a woman, you have to be wise and know what your partner can and cannot handle.

5. When you get married, try to keep part of your life separate from your husband's, meaning have your own friends and hobbies. When I got married, I left all my friends and family and moved to a new place. I even started attending his church. It was all new to me, so I clung to the person I knew the best, Bill. Maybe he felt smothered. Do not let your whole life be focused on him, only because if he goes it will feel like your whole life goes with him.

CHAPTER 4

Facing Infidelity

Sometimes the heart needs time to accept
what the mind already knows.
—*Unknown*

Infidelity is universal and has its horns in every facet of society: rich or poor, Christian or non-Christian, whatever race.

Instead of getting better, things were getting worse. Though I was trying desperately to fix things with Bill, nothing seemed to work. Bill was showing no interest in me—on the contrary, he kept pulling further and further away.

Sometimes I saw him with such a faraway look, deep in thought, I'd ask him out of concern to tell me what he was thinking. But he would just say, "It's OK."

I don't know about you, but I really like it when my partner opens up to me, feeling comfortable sharing his deepest thoughts. To me it's a very important form of intimacy.

Have you ever thought: *I would pay a lot of money just to know exactly what X is thinking?* Or, *A penny for your thoughts?* I so much wanted him to share with me.

Bill's reaction to our second son

During all this I was still pregnant. While pregnant with my first son, I remember, laughter filled our home. I love to laugh, so much so that I watched a lot of sitcoms. The effect of that was that my son grew up loving to laugh and watch sitcoms.

Now, for my second pregnancy, I was not working but at home crying a river all day, drowning in depression and sadness. I asked God to help this not to negatively impact my unborn baby.

After birth, he cried for everything. This was frustrating, but my mind would revert to what happened while pregnant, which helped me be more patient.

But Bill hardly even picked him up.

This was quite obvious to not just me but some of his family members as well.

One day I got up at the crack of dawn. Why? Because it was a special occasion. We were all going to the beach with Bill's family: his mom, dad, brothers, sister, nieces, nephews, and other in-laws.

Excited because since the birth of our second son I hardly got to go anywhere, I carefully packed our bags, careful to put in swimwear, clothes, towels, and the baby necessities.

After that, I grated some cheese and made a paste by adding a bit of butter and mustard and grated a little piece of onion in it, then mixed everything together. I did basically the same thing with a tin of corn beef.

Then I spread the paste on one slice of bread, and placing another slice on top of that, I gently patted them together.

After which I carefully cut off the crust. Then cut the cheese sandwiches into triangles and the beef ones into rectangles.

I neatly packed them in a bag with water and some snacks. I didn't have to cook food because we planned to cook on the beach.

It was time to leave, and we packed the vehicle and were on our way.

The sky was clear. The sun was shining in all its glory through the vehicle windows. A perfect day for a beach picnic.

My spirit quickly deflated like the air flowing from a balloon when I saw Brooke there. A specially invited guest.

Her husband was still overseas working, so she came with her son.

However, what hurt me the most was not Brooke's presence but the reaction of Bill to our second son.

He hardly touched or interacted with him.

I was very worried about how his father's apparent antipathy to him would impact his life. I didn't want him to grow up with a father who had doubts about being his father. *Could that be at issue?* So, one day I broached the subject.

I suggested that he should take a DNA test since it was quite clear he didn't think he was the father.

It was one of the most painful things I ever had to do because it was patently absurd to need a DNA test done to prove to my husband, he was the father.

It was like my heart was a piece of glass, and someone smashed it on the ground, breaking it into many pieces.

However, better for me to feel this pain of brokenness than for my son to. The last thing I wanted was for him to grow up with a father who treated him differently from his elder brother.

I told my husband I would even go with him to the test because I knew he was the only one I'd had sex with, there was no way on earth our child could not be his.

When we met, as he knew, I was a virgin. We had sex the first time on our wedding night, which was self-evident. That was one of the things I was thankful to God for, that I had kept my promise to him.

At first, Bill rejected the need for a DNA test, but later he came back and said he would do it. At the time, we were told that our son was too young for such a test. We had to wait until he reached six months.

Time to look for a new job

I began to wonder: *What would happen if Bill left me now?*

I knew I would be in a lot of trouble financially. I had no job. *How will I survive? Will he still give me money for the bills, etc?*

After thinking this through, I decided to start looking for a job. Without mentioning it to him, I sent out a number of applications. Not long after that, I got a job.

This is when I told Bill about my decision to find employment. He was not very pleased and reminded me that we had decided that I would not work until the baby was one year old. Our son was almost four months.

As much as I would have loved to stay home a bit longer, I knew in myself why I was doing this, to help establish my financial stability. However, I never shared this explanation with Bill.

He realized that my mind was made up, so we hired a babysitter and I started working in December 2007.

Our anniversary cruise

Each year, Bill and I took turns planning our anniversary.

In January 2008 it was a big milestone for us, ten years. I wanted it to be spectacular and memorable. And it was my turn to choose what we would do. *Why not an island-hopping day cruise to the Grenadines?*

Let me tell you a bit more about the Grenadines. It is a tropical paradise for yachting, scuba diving, enjoying nature, and relaxing in luxurious hideaways.

The Grenadines is also blessed with warm, friendly people, beautiful white-sand beaches, lush tropical landscapes, and crystal-clear turquoise waters. They're known for their yacht-filled harbors and sailing spots, like the reef-lined island of Bequia, with secluded Princess Margaret Beach and the Old Hegg Turtle Sanctuary.

One of my hobbies is just to be around nature. I find it very therapeutic and calming; hence, the reason I chose this trip.

The day came. And after journeying to the Kingstown Port, we boarded the yacht. As I looked around me, I saw other couples beaming with excitement.

I should let you know a little about me. I do not like boats. Why? Because I get seasick. All the tossing up and down, side to side on the water makes me feel as though the food in my stomach wants to make a run to my mouth and out.

So why plan a cruise, then? I wanted this celebration to be spectacular, remember, and nothing could top this.

To avoid being sick, about an hour before departure I took some Gravol tablets, which usually worked.

The ropes were loosened from the wharf, and off we went. One hour into our journey we arrived at Port Elizabeth in the seven-square-mile island of Bequia, our first stop.

Every time I go to Bequia something transforms me. No matter what the beach is, they are all beautiful. That day was no different as we sunbathed and took a swim. We also indulged in a short journey to the Old Hegg Turtle

Sanctuary, where we paid a fee to be up close to the large and small turtles, interacting with and even touching them. It was amazing!

The purpose of the sanctuary is to safely get the turtles past the dangerous moment after birth, when they would be prey to birds, then nurture them for six months to three years, and return them to the wild. Meanwhile, they live in mostly small concrete pools.

Our next stop was Mustique, where my aunt lives—a private island with luxury villas and quiet beaches. Celebrities like Mick Jagger, Bryan Adams, and Tommy Hilfiger all own homes there.

As we strolled along Britannia Bay beach, hand in hand, two lovebirds, suddenly I gazed my eyes across to an exquisite site. I wished I had wings to immediately fly there. What I saw appeared to be a cluster of island huts; multiple small hutlike buildings with pointed roofs—overlooking the calm, even rippleless, water. They started on the beach and went straight into the sea as though they were floating.

It was like nothing I have ever seen before.

As I walked closer, the suspense was beginning to get the better of me. I had to ask, what is that?

Bill quickly replied, "Basil's Bar, a bar and restaurant." Later I learnt that Bon Jovi, Mick Jagger, and other celebrities performed there, and it was also the site of the Mustique Blues Festival.

Next, we sailed to Canouan.

This day was just getting better and better.

I wondered where we were heading next.

It turned out to be picturesque.

Looking around, I could see nature at its purest, no roads or buildings in sight. We were in the Tobago Cays Marine Park, famous for its coral reefs. I could see other yachts dotting the sea.

"Who wants to swim with the turtles?" we were all asked. Both Bill and I plunged into the warm turquoise water, diving underwater to catch a glimpse of the turtles and swimming side by side with them.

It was magical!

I wanted to stay there forever, but it was time to hop to another island—the Palm Island, a private island with its own hotel and spa. Lots of coconut trees along the beach provided an exclusive hideaway.

Do you know the expression, "time flies when you are having fun"?

That is exactly what was happening, but we had one more island to explore, Mayreau.

As the yacht drew closer to shore I looked down into the water; to my surprise the water was so clear I could see starfish on the ocean floor. I had never seen them before except on TV.

On the beach locals were selling souvenirs, like T-shirts, bracelets, and sandals. Off we went to find a secluded area on the beach just to be alone. Then we lay on the silky white sand, looking up at the clear blue sky above us, enjoying each other and nature.

At long last. This trip was the first time we had been able to go out after the birth of our second son, now four months old. Oh, how I longed for and missed our date times.

As they say, "All good things must come to an end." Time to head back to real life and everything that comes with it.

What a happy day that was, which I wanted never to end.

The DNA test

Our second son was now six months old so we decided to have the DNA test done.

On the day of the test, I felt so broken inside that I couldn't bring myself to go. When he came back, I asked him how it went and if our son cried.

He said no because they just took a swab from his mouth and that no needles were involved. Fortunately.

The day we expected to get the results I went to his office. He was seated at his desk. I sat on the chair directly in front of him and asked, "Have you received the test result?" He said yes, then grew silent. With piercing eyes, I asked him, "What did it say?" He said, "The child is mine." He said it as though he was disappointed, with absolutely no sign of relief or excitement. At least, he didn't lie.

I was not amazed; I'd known for over a year now he was looking for a way to say I was cheating too. So, a test that proved his paternity was not what he wanted to see.

He handed me the result. It confirmed a 99.99 percent chance he was the father. *How could he deny those results, 99.99 percent?* Believe it or not, afterwards, I immediately saw a completely different attitude from him towards our son.

It was only from that point that he started being the father he needed to be to him.

Despite all the pain this situation caused me, the pain was worth it.

Bill counseling another couple

A friend of mine knew her husband was cheating. However, she had no proof. She prayed to God about it and specifically asked Him to show her proof.

One day God led her to find a diary, in which her husband wrote sizzling details of times spent together with the other woman. Her suspicions were right.

In an attempt to save her marriage, unaware I was facing the same issues, she called Bill to talk to her husband.

I had told no one, not even my mother, what was happening to me. I was going through this alone, all alone. I have been a very independent and private person since I was a child. I liked to handle things on my own. Besides, I had no proof of anything.

God was the only one I talked to about it.

I couldn't bring myself to confide in her. Unlike her I had no diary.

I accompanied him to visit the couple. The way he spoke to him made me even more suspicious. When she complained about what was happening and that he was taking their child to this woman's home, Bill took the husband's side.

He was not talking about what God expects but said, "It's his child, so he can take her wherever he wants."

He could not bring himself to condemn the behavior. This was yet another occasion that made my suspicions of his affair seem even more likely.

Just being there in that conversation, hearing what this lady was going through, knowing I was going through the very same thing, my heart was silently aching inside.

Looking back now, I wonder, with the phone bill and everything that was going on with them, *what more proof was I looking for? Did I have to catch them in the act?*

I am sure even to you that they were having an affair is clear.

I loved him so much, my mind was having a mighty hard time convincing my heart of the obvious.

Other Women

Several years back, an incident happened at our home with my elder son's babysitter. Having spent the whole day out, we had just returned from a church function.

When we arrived, my son was sleeping, so I lifted him up out of the car and went inside. I was the first person upstairs. It was just starting to get dark, but I could still see. So, I didn't put on the light. I sat down on the sofa in the living room there, taking off my son's shoes and clothes.

Coming up next, the babysitter passed me. I don't think she saw where I was. She went into the guest room to put some stuff down and walked back out. No one put on the light yet. My husband came up the stairs at the same time. They met in the middle of the living room.

I just saw she went right up to him and put her arms around his neck, bringing her lips to his to kiss him. I don't know if he saw me, but he took her hands off his neck and pushed her away.

All this was happening right in front of my eyes. I was very disturbed about it.

I spoke to Bill. He said nothing was happening between them.

Now, this young lady was practically living in our home, taking care of our son. *How could I feel comfortable, having her here after what I saw that night?* I expressed my feelings to my husband, and he left it up to me.

I spoke to her about how I felt, and I let her go. She later wrote a letter to me, saying that I was like a mother to her and that nothing was going on. I didn't hold her as an enemy, but I just couldn't have her staying in my home anymore.

When I mentioned this to one of my friends, she asked, *"What will you do if Bill is cheating?"* I told her I would try and work things out.

Many years later she confessed to me that there was no doubt in her mind that he was cheating at that time, but she hadn't known how to tell me.

Another time I found an email from a woman asking him, *"Why are we not going out anymore?"* It was one of his client's employees.

He would have been to this office several times and had taken me there as well. To this date I never mentioned it to him.

The fact that she was now asking that question made me think that maybe he had stopped seeing her.

There were rumors going around our neighbourhood between yet another young lady from our church and Bill. I noticed her calling him very often. When I asked him about it, he gave his standby answer: that she was going through some issues and he was trying to help. The matter was even taken before the church board—a platform for pastoral staff and church members to make decisions on issues affecting the church.

Looking back, was I being naive in dealing with these matters? *If I had dealt with them differently—gotten to the bottom of these early warning signs that he had the tendencies of a philanderer—would it have made a difference as to what was happening now? Was he an incurable womanizer?*

Daily Devotions

We were still having devotions together in the mornings while lying in bed. I remember some sections in one of the devotional books talked about how a husband should treat his wife. I could see Bill stirring uneasily, listening to the advice. He even made a remark: "That's what you want to hear."

Does reading daily devotions mean that someone is truly connected to God and is doing His will? Definitely not. A lot of people go through the motions, but their heart is far from God.

The incident at work; Can I have a kiss?

Despite the fact that I was very unhappy, I never once strayed but remained faithful to my wedding vows.

Working, I found myself keeping late hours to meet monthly deadlines—being in charge of the financial statements, which were due by the tenth of each month. Many times, I was all alone in the office.

However, on one such occasion, in October 2008, my boss was working late also. Standing by a cabinet, I was shuffling through some files when he suddenly came up next to me, started a conversation, and asked flirtatiously, "Can I have a kiss?"

This was quite a shock. He was someone I worked with in a previous employment, and nothing of this sort ever happened.

He was now in front of me, asking me for a kiss. I said in no uncertain terms, "No." He asked, "Are you sure that is what you want to say?" The tone sounded like a threat. I said, "Yes." Thinking of Joseph in the Bible who fled the scene when Potiphar's wife, married to his Egyptian master, made an all-too-clear pass at him; immediately, I closed the cabinet, packed my stuff, and left the office.

I mentioned nothing to anybody, not even Bill.

That night I thought about the incident. I knew that my boss was not happy with my response and was going to try and make my life at work difficult. I decided there and then that it was not wise for me to stay there.

At work the next day I carried out my duties as a professional. I did not mention anything to him about the incident, and neither did he bring it up.

However, not long after that there was a yearly performance review, and he gave me a bad report. No surprise there.

It did not take me long to find a new job. By November 17, 2008, I was on a plane traveling to St. Lucia for an interview. Thankfully, I got the job. They had a branch in St. Vincent, at an office a lot closer to home, which would allow me more time to spend with my kids.

God had once again turned a negative to a positive as he promised in Romans 8:28.

Informing my boss I was leaving, I handed in my two months' notice.

It was close to the time bonuses were given out, and he did not give any to me, saying bonuses were for current employees.

Brooke and I pregnant at the same time

With me still not willing to accept that an affair was going on, Bill and I had a vibrant sex life. At times he was playful and amorous and made advances to me, which I caved in to. It wasn't just him. Sometimes I initiated. He loved sex, and so did I. The fact that he was a long-distance runner and gave multiple orgasms, *how could I resist?*

About a year after the birth of our second son I got pregnant again. We went to the doctor together, a normal thing for us to do, even now, harking back to the days when we did almost everything together.

The doctor confirmed I was pregnant. When we came out of the office, my husband grabbed and hugged me and said he was excited about the baby, which might be surprising to you after the way he was distant with our second son.

In January 2010, I noticed that Brooke's tummy was looking large, so I asked him if she was pregnant. He said, "Yes." I then asked, "Why did you not tell me?"

He said, "I knew you would make a big thing out of it, and I didn't want any confusion." You see things were fine with us as long as Brooke was not being mentioned.

At that point my mind reflected back on a few months before, when I had a miscarriage. It is then I realized that my onetime best friend and I were pregnant at the same time. *Could it be by the same man—my husband?*

She had her baby in April 2010, while mine, if still alive, would have been born a few months after.

My Miscarriages

Being pregnant is mostly a happy occasion but can turn into sadness when it ends abruptly in a miscarriage.

Many women go through miscarriages, an experience that they find to be heart-breaking. Some even become depressed and feel less than a woman.

Looking back on my two miscarriages, I could have left the marriage with four instead of two children. I really felt miserable when I had my first miscarriage, thinking it might have been a girl and we would have had the pair: a boy and a girl.

I recall we were so excited, sharing the news. It was not a good feeling, telling people I had a miscarriage.

My second miscarriage was months before Bill's confession.

Once again God, knowing the future, worked things out in this way. Thank you, God!

Bill tried to get me pregnant

I had not been on the pill or any long-term contraceptive for a while but used both the safety period and withdrawal methods.

However, once before having sex, I knew it was not inside the safety period. I told him, and he said he didn't want to use a condom and decided we would use the withdrawal method, but in the end, I noticed he didn't withdraw.

Knowing how things were between us, I didn't want to be left alone with three children. I had decided to make sure I didn't get another in case he left me.

So, the very next day bright and early before going into work, I went to the pharmacy and bought the morning-after pill.

A couple of weeks later Bill asked, "Did you buy the morning pill?"

I guess he was waiting to hear me say I missed my period or I was pregnant. I told him, "Yes, I did."

It dawned on me that he was probably deliberately trying to get me pregnant. Maybe he thought if I got pregnant, I would not leave him when the truth finally came out.

I knew with all my heart that God's timing is always the perfect timing. God's delay is not His denial. It was only a matter of time before the truth was known.

Encounter with Joe

One day I encountered Joe in a supermarket in St. Vincent. I asked, "Why didn't you respond to me that day in the garden in Trinidad? Because of that my husband accused me of having an affair with you."

He said he hadn't seen me and that "what God has put together, let no man put asunder." Then he asked me what

I thought was the strangest thing: "Are you sure he's not cheating on you?"

My breathing changed for a moment. However, I did not make him wise because I had "no proof"—still in the land of denial. *What more was I waiting for?*

How do you know if your partner is having an affair?

I would be pretending if I said I have all the answers to this question, but I can share with you from my own experience twelve reasons I had concluded my husband was cheating on me with my best friend. They happened over the span of about three years but not in any chronological order:

1. Taking his phone everywhere

After my return from studying, one of the first changes I noticed in my husband was with his phone. He was now always on his phone and took it everywhere he went in the house, even when going to the toilet.

This was not the case before; he used to leave his phone lying about anywhere.

I mentioned the change. "It is my phone, and I can do whatever I want with it," he said with a condescending tone.

Before, we knew each other's phone password and would answer the other's phone, if necessary, but that was all changing now.

A sure sign that he was definitely hiding something.

2. Beginning to find fault with me

I went from being the best wife to the worst. He started to find all kinds of faults and implemented outrageous demands on me.

All of a sudden, he started telling me I needed to clean the toilets and house every day, I wasn't cooking as much as I should, etc.

He started comparing me to his mother, who, he said, cleaned the toilet every day. A woman who was a housewife most of her life having no need to work and had no young children to take care of.

At the time I was working full time having to work late to meet deadlines, had two young kids to look after, having to do homework with one every day plus house chores. Bill, by contrast, came home late every night. Mostly after 10 p.m. or 11 p.m.

I told him I needed help, it was too much for me, that we needed to hire a cleaner to come in at least once a week.

I remember telling him that, "I am not a superwoman."

At one point, he rebuked me, "Are you vexed that God made you a woman?"

I often say, "Life is so unfair and harder for women"; we are expected to fill both our female role and the man's role in the home: doing the cooking, the ironing, the cleaning, and looking after the kids. In addition, to go out and work—many of us having a fulltime job to help meet the financial obligations of the family.

Sadly, a lot of men act like they are doing the woman a favor whenever they do something in the home. I think it's high time that the men level up and assist more in the homes. What do you think?

We had the money to hire someone, but for some reason he was refusing, insisting that I do everything. Eventually we hired someone.

3. Refusing to go out with me

When your husband has reached the point of not wanting to go out with you anymore, it can be a sure sign that he is drawing further and further away from you and closer into the arms of another woman.

Our date night on Tuesdays continued over into our marriage because we were in love and wanted to make sure we did everything within our power to have a happy marriage.

So, we religiously kept to our date, missing it only on rare occasions.

However, now he went so far as to tell me, "I don't feel comfortable going out with you anymore." But never giving a reason as to why he didn't want to.

4. Making unusual requests

Look for any unusual change in behavior. It does not have to be only connected to sex but can be—for example, not wanting to go out with you, as just mentioned.

I had not been using any long-term birth control, but we were using the safety-period method, as mentioned, and condoms outside of that time.

However, at one point, he started requesting to use condoms during sex even inside the safety period. This happened only a few times. I just brushed it off saying, "We don't need to."

He absolutely hated to use them.

This request really puzzled me. *Why the sudden change?* But I kept it to myself. In the back of my mind, I thought maybe he was being told by Brooke to do that. Or it could have been something else. I will never know his reasoning.

5. No interest in having sex with me

A lot of the times when this happens in a relationship, your partner is getting his pleasure with someone else.

For a period, Bill no longer showed interest in having sex with me; three months went by.

All this made me feel so sad and depressed. For many days I just stayed home and cried because I felt unwanted and undesired by my husband.

However, his lack of interest in sex with me did not last, and having sex was never a real issue. I saw it as his way of coming back to me, which I welcomed with open arms.

6. Forgetting special occasions

Forgetting special occasions can be a sure sign that your husband is preoccupied elsewhere, maybe with another woman who now consumes his mind.

In 2009, Bill forgot my birthday. First time in eleven years of marriage. His newfound love was now occupying so much of his thoughts that he was starting to forget me.

It was not surprising to me but was really hard to come to grips with—yet another confirmation of my suspicions of his unfaithfulness.

I decided to say nothing. Days passed. I still said nothing.

One day he came home in a panic. "I can't believe that I forgot your birthday. I was driving and stopped in the middle of the road when I realized the date and that your birthday had passed more than a week before."

The next day he gave me a foot spa. It was the last birthday present I received from him.

When I told Brooke about it, she said, "If it was me, I would not have forgiven him." I am not sure why I even mentioned it to her.

7. Being away from home more

As mentioned before, he came home very late almost every night with the excuse that he was working.

Lying in bed, I would wait up for him because I just couldn't fall asleep while he was out. I needed to know that he was safe.

The way our bedroom was situated, I could see when he was driving into our yard. In fact, I would hear the sound of the vehicle from yards away and the sound of the gate opening as it slid across its tracks even before the jeep reached our gate.

The gate was automatic and had a remote.

Brooke lived on a hill in a house visible from our bedroom window, even from the bed.

On several occasions when I heard his jeep approach, I looked up that hill and saw her vehicle driving into her yard at the same time.

Was that a coincidence? I'd have to be pretty much an idiot to think so.

When I mentioned it to him, he objected, "How do you know it was her in the vehicle? It could be her brother."

He got defensive and accused me of always wanting to make confusion in the marriage.

Not only was he coming home late from work, but he was also out a lot during weekends. At one point while I was not working, he started to do some farming to help generate extra income.

However, many times he left very early in the morning, before daylight, and—almost as though he was trying to avoid being at home—never came back until very late.

I have no doubt in my mind that he used some of this time to be with Brooke. *How could I believe otherwise?*

8. Refusing to work together to save the relationship

Despite everything, I was quite emotional about wanting to save the marriage.

One day while we were traveling home together, I pleaded, "We need to come together to work on our marriage."

"You do what you need to do to fix your part and I will fix mine," he responded abruptly.

I found that a very odd thing to say, knowing that in a marriage both parties have to work together. "There is no you and me but us when it comes to these matters," I objected.

This was definitely not a *you do your own thing and I do mine* moment.

It was like he was speaking a foreign language to me because we were accustomed to working together in all aspects of our lives.

Was he finding it hard to do what he knew as a Christian he should?

9. Starting to say "mine" instead of "ours"

Before, we were both saying "ours." Now he had taken to saying "mine" instead.

It was now "my house," "my business," my vehicle."

I would listen in silence, and my heart would ache not because of fear of potentially losing these things but the mere thought of losing my husband.

Although he was there physically, in his mind he was already separating himself from me and gravitating more to someone else, Brooke.

These are outward actions, sometimes done unconsciously, that indicate something is very wrong in a relationship.

10. Looking for a way out

One Saturday afternoon after church we came home for lunch.

Bill was on the bed, lying down, looking very studious, at his laptop. When I came in, I asked him, "What are you doing?"

"I am researching about divorce," he replied.

Well, this made it clear to me. I wasn't surprised. I said, "Let me join you."

Wow, my response was even shocking to me.

What would have been your reaction to this situation, knowing full well that your husband was thinking of divorcing you?

I took him to Matthew 19 and read from verse 1 down to 9, when Jesus said, "And I say unto you, whosoever shall put away his wife, except it be for fornication, and shall marry another, committeth adultery: and whoso marrieth her which is put away doth commit adultery."

Awhile back, at a church leadership function, he told me they were saying that the guilty party could remarry as well if the innocent party got remarried because at that point the vow was broken.

"Where is that in the Bible?" I asked, but he could not tell me.

I think that news made a shift in his mind, and he started to look at divorce as an option.

Could this be the reason why the divorce rate in the church is as high as out of the church?

11. Tested positive for a Sexually Transmitted Disease (STD)

If you find yourself with an STD and you know that you have been faithful to your partner, this could mean that you are being cheated on.

I found myself in a very peculiar situation.

I had been having a discharge for years, which started after the birth of my first child, even while in Trinidad, and my doctor could not detect why. I would be given treatment, which seemed to work, but after a while the symptom reappeared. That was the cycle, and I was getting very frustrated—until one day after returning from studying, when Bill and I went to the doctor and I voiced my frustration to her. She then decided to test for chlamydia—an STD.

She sent Bill outside and proceeded to ask me if I thought that Bill was cheating on me.

Not very comfortable talking to her about my suspicions—I saw her as my doctor, not my therapist—I said nothing.

Coming from a small, underdeveloped country and well over ten years ago, the test took one month to return the results.

It was positive.

Fortunately, it could be easily treated with medication, which the doctor prescribed and I started taking; unlike some women who end up with incurable disease like HIV (Human Immunodeficiency Virus).

At that point the doctor decided to test Bill. I don't know why she did not test him the same time as me.

Anyway, we waited another month, and his test came back negative. To me this was straight out of *The Twilight Zone*. It made absolutely no sense. Bill was the only man I'd had sex with, and we were having sex without the use of condoms. How could I be positive and he negative?

Searching for answers, I went to a male gynecologist this time. When I explained the scenario, he told me that some husbands, finding out they have a STD, do not tell their wife anything.

Instead, they go to a pharmacist friend and get treatment unbeknownst to the wife. However, when the wife starts getting symptoms and goes to the doctor to get tested, she'll be positive.

When he is now tested, he's negative.

Shocked by my findings, I went to yet another male gynecologist, and lo and behold he told me the same thing without me telling him what the other doctor said.

Have you ever seen the comedy *Why Did I Get Married?* It came out October 12, 2007. In it, refusing to tell his wife anything, Marcus asked his doctor friend, Terry, for a shot for the "burns."

Was Bill the kind of person who would do such a thing? This was the reality, but I did not know it.

He had a whole month to go and get treatment without me knowing anything. After all, he knew what test I had done.

Despite everything else that was going on with Bill and Brooke, I just could not bring myself to believe that he was capable of such a thing. I never once disclosed my findings to Bill.

So, I continued to look for other reasons to explain my predicament.

Meanwhile, of course, he was deceitfully accusing me of being unfaithful, even though he knew the truth. I maintained my innocence and tried to assure Bill I'd never cheated.

This was a mystery to me for quite a long time in the marriage.

12. Unusual bank withdrawals or purchases

When Bill and I got married we opted for only one bank account, where we would consolidate our earnings.

If you and your partner share a bank account, make sure you closely monitor it for any unusual withdrawal or purchases. This is very important.

I am sure we all have seen a movie where the wife finds maybe a purchase from a jewelry or lingerie shop yet didn't receive any such gift.

In my case, it was a check withdrawal of $10,000, very large relative to our finances, written in Bill's name, from our business account—a withdrawal I knew nothing of.

When I pressed him about it, "I sent it to my parents to help with my dad's surgery," he explained.

I was aware that his dad was overseas, seeking medical attention for his eyes. *However, did I just believe him?*

Oh no.

I called his dad and asked, "Did Bill send $10,000 for you?" Surprisingly, he said no, with a bit of a confused sound in his voice.

Then I asked his mother; she said, yes.

Was she telling the truth, or covering for her favorite son? I never spoke to Bill about these conversations.

Who did I believe, the dad or the mom?

Whether I was right or not, I leaned toward believing the dad.

So, what did Bill do with all that money?

Did he have a secret bank account?

Was he now setting aside funds in preparation for his future with Brooke?

Was he planning to leave me?

How much more can I bear?

Will I ever get to know the truth?

So many questions; having no answers made me feel even more insecure in the relationship.

I felt like I was sitting on a time bomb, not knowing when it would detonate.

One day a lady from the church made a comment to me, "You got the last good man." I just smiled.

Another time a young woman from church approached me and said, "You have it all: the husband, the house, and the kids." So, it looked from the outside. Again, I just smiled. If only she knew what I was going through behind closed doors.

What other people see is not necessarily a true picture of what is really happening in someone's life.

Lessons Learned

1. *Some men when they are cheating try to get their partner pregnant. They do this to deter her from leaving (thinking the woman might not want to leave the relationship, being pregnant, with a young child or having a certain number of kids). Be very careful and protect yourself from getting pregnant if you are seeing any signs of infidelity.*

2. *Don't fully depend on your partner for everything. Ensure that you put yourself in a position financially where if he leaves today, you can still take care of yourself.*

3. *As mothers and women, we should educate, enlighten, and provide guidance to girls about men and life on the whole so they can make better choices when they choose a partner.*

CHAPTER 5

The Confession

Better to be hurt by the
truth than to be comforted by lies.
—Khaled Hosseini

Monday, February 22, 2010, started like any other day. I woke up, had devotion with Bill and got the kids ready for school.

I was upstairs with the kids, brushing their teeth, bathing and dressing them, while Bill was in the kitchen, preparing breakfast for us all.

I later realized that he used these times to call Brooke.

After work, I strolled across to our business office, less than five minutes' walk from my office, to prepare the Value Added Tax (VAT) document I did monthly.

Everybody had left already, so I used my keys to open the door, walked up the stairs, went straight to Bill's office, and sat down at his desk to start working.

As soon as I opened his laptop, I saw his cell phone bill on the screen.

I had noticed before that since December 2006, when I discovered the snail-mail bill that created havoc and opened this book, his phone bill was no longer arriving by mail.

I remember I asked, "How come your phone bills are not coming in the mail?"

"The phone company called me and said they are no longer mailing out the bills but sending them via email," he responded.

This I didn't believe but just stayed silent.

Sometimes it is best not to say anything and let people think they've outsmarted you. This way, you get to see their true colours and learn who you are really dealing with.

Anyway, when I looked at the bill, I noticed that very familiar number again.

You guessed it!

It was Brooke's. On weekends they made calls that lasted forty-five minutes up to an hour sometimes.

I was fuming inside and thinking: *They are working together and seeing each other every weekday. Why on earth does he need to be calling her on weekends for that length of time? Are they just unable to stay out of touch with each other for even a few hours?*

I was convinced in that moment without a shadow of a doubt that this had to be more than just friends.

Without even thinking, I picked up the phone.

"Where are you?" I asked Bill. A question I've asked hundreds of times.

"I am at a client's office, and no one else is here," he said.

Something that was not strange for me to hear because he was well trusted by his clients; they would leave him alone in their office after working hours for him to work.

Feeling overwhelmed with emotions and not having the strength to hold back the true intent of my call, I blurted out, "Why do you have to call Brooke on weekends? You are seeing her every day at work. I am coming there right now to see you and I need to know the truth."

Confession of infidelity

He was working on a computer at one of the desks. When I arrived, he barely acknowledged my presence.

I got straight to the point. "Tell me the truth. Are you having an affair with Brooke?" I asked it in a very firm but somewhat trembling tone of voice.

"We kissed," he confessed.

"Did you have sex with her?"

He replied, "Just once."

"Is the baby yours?" I asked, determined there and then to get to the bottom of matters.

He gave me a kind of look. "You waited a long time to ask me that question."

He was sure right about that.

It was only because I didn't want to cause an argument, why I never asked the question until now.

"It is her husband's baby," he answered.

Did that news bring any real relief to me?

No, I was just not sure whether to believe it or not and took it with a grain of salt.

Maybe it was because during the whole conversation his mannerism was calm, and he was talking as someone might about the weather—as though he had been waiting a long time to have this conversation.

However, it was not important enough for him to stop what he was doing; he just kept on with his work. He showed no emotions, no sign of remorse; he didn't even ask for forgiveness or say he was sorry.

There was no effort on his part to try and console or comfort me. No empathy. I was left on my own to deal with the situation however I could.

With that cruel realization of what kind of person Bill really was, I believed then and there that he was capable of doing what the doctors had told me about three years ago: to take treatment for the STD behind my back.

My heart was bleeding, I was in so much pain mentally and emotionally and unsure what my next move should be.

As I stood there in the middle of that office, questions began flooding my mind. *What should I say? And how do I react?*

How should one react after finding out that that one thing you fear the most in your life is indeed true? What do you do when your life falls apart?

Even if I was standing on a white sandy beach surrounded by clear blue waters with no cloud in the sky, it would not have made any difference whatsoever. The fact is, when your world is falling apart, it doesn't matter where it happens; the impact is devastating.

Having had my suspicions since 2006, for over three years, I would be prepared for this moment, you are thinking. But I couldn't stop holding onto that little glimmer of hope. All this time. Maybe, just maybe, somehow, nothing was really going on, I had told myself without logically believing it. But still . . .

I could no longer hang on to that hope. It was now ripped out of my grasp.

It was all out in the open.

In a way I was glad that, finally, I knew the truth because for years I felt I was being manipulated to think what I could all but prove was ridiculous and farfetched.

I'd questioned my sanity so many times ("Maybe they were really just friends").

Other times their relationship defied any attempt to pretend.

For years I was spinning round and round in the mud, going nowhere, having no concrete proof. Not knowing what to do.

I recall many times telling Bill, "The Bible cannot lie": "Whatever is in darkness must come to light" (Luke 12:2-3). That day had finally come, like a thief in the night.

"Everything in the dark must come to light because God cannot lie. So, if anything is happening between you, one day it will all come out," I continued.

This, I told him several times, but wishing in the back of my mind I were wrong; that is, that nothing was going on. However, the signs didn't lie; they were all there.

Also, I used to tell him, "You can do whatever you want but not for as long as you want. At some point God will step in and say, "enough is enough."

My mind retreated to just the very night before, when my heart was racing under the bed sheets while Bill and I made sweet, passionate love. Neither of us had the least thought then that that was the last time. I was standing there, staring at the man I'd never make love with again.

We had used the last condom, and earlier that same day I went to buy more.

That same morning, we had devotion together, like every day. Never did I guess that truth would be staring me right in the face hours later.

Bought a new vehicle

It was just a few months back, in November 2009, we bought another vehicle at a price of $85,000.

The company I worked with was selling it. Initially all the paperwork was put in my name.

But Bill played on my emotions, reminding me I wanted us to do things together and work on our marriage. He behaved as though things were going to be fine—effectively pulling the wool over my eyes. And once again, I had failed to see what was really happening.

So, I foolishly added his name, forgetting at that point that our house, valued at $500,000, was in his name only (he got the land we built on from his grandmother).

Brooke would have been about four months' pregnant at the time, but he just said what he said to manipulate me to get what he wanted.

I kept second guessing myself about their relationship: *Am I seeing things that are not there? Am I being overly dramatic? Maybe I am being too jealous, as Bill suggested.*

Many people second guess their view of reality after getting into a fight with their partner. After being giving an alternate explanation of what happened.

Was I a victim of gaslighting?

Gaslighting is a manipulative tactic used by people to gain control in a relationship. It's making someone seem or feel unstable, irrational, not credible, making them feel like what they're seeing or experiencing isn't real, that they're imagining it, that no one else will believe them. It undermines victim's sense of being in the driving seat of their own actions.

Looking back, I can say without a doubt that I was.

These are some tactics in gaslighting, some of which I personally experienced. See if you can spot those that relate to me:

- **Invalidating your feelings** ("You are so insensitive." "You are overreacting. You are too jealous.")

- **Devaluing your worth** ("You are stupid." "You cannot possibly understand.")

- **Denying the truth** ("Are you sure this happened? You don't remember things clearly, anyway. How do you know she was the one driving her vehicle? We are just friends.")

- **Blaming you for the partner's actions** ("Don't get upset over nonsensical things and I won't get angry at you. You are always bringing this up just to cause confusion.")

If this sounds familiar to you, you might also be a victim of gaslighting. In that case, what do you do about it?

First, identify the signs.

Secondly, speak up and be assertive. Let your partner know how his behavior is affecting you. When you are being called a liar, maybe reply by saying, "Let us agree to disagree."

As I think back, I conclude that Bill wanted to keep both Brooke and me.

Was he torn between two lovers? Didn't want to choose? Or did he love his wife but loved having fun on the side? Maybe it was a case where he probably felt like a "king," knowing he was having sex with two women.

On the hunt for Brooke

I left Bill in the office and drove over forty minutes, straight to Brooke's house. *Why? What would I say to her? Would my emotions stifle my words and strike me temporarily dumb?*

No, I didn't intend a crime of passion. As I said before, I can't physically fight.

She was out, but I met her mom there and recounted what had happened. While talking to her on the porch, I was standing next to a washing machine, which I hit in anger.

She said, "You will have to talk to her about it."

Trying to save my marriage

I then went home and waited for Bill. This night, he was early.

When he arrived, we discussed what happened. My first instinct was not to get a divorce. Even at this point I wanted to save my marriage. After all, I believed Bill was the love of my life.

I spoke to him as a Christian to a Christian and reminded him about the scriptures and what God expected of him. All he said was, "There is nothing you could tell me that I don't know already."

I spoke to him as a wife to a husband, reminding him of the marriage vows we made many years ago, "till death do us part."

I pleaded with him, desperately trying to draw him back to me.

That night my eyes stayed wide open.

Confronting Brooke

The truth dribbled out.

The next day I passed by the office, spotting Brooke inside. I told her, "I know."

She said, "I didn't do anything you didn't do."

"I didn't have sex with somebody else's husband. You did," I fired back. She said, "So?" putting some attitude in the tone of her voice.

Unable to comprehend what I was hearing, I took one step backward. In wonderment, I thought: *Is this really a Christian woman talking here?* There was absolutely no remorse.

It was the worst betrayal imaginable.

I was certainly not expecting such ruthlessness.

Not very long after that, her sister and mother came into the office. She had called for reinforcements. I was all alone, with no one on my side, feeling outnumbered.

After a while I just left to go back to work.

That night I told my husband she would have to leave the office. I told him he had to choose.

I made it very clear to him again that I had no intention of sharing my husband with anyone; it was either me alone or not me at all.

I also said, "If you decide to leave, I can make it without you."

I often wondered: *Did I do the right thing?* I said it because I wanted him to stay with me only because he loved me and wanted to stay, not for any other reason.

I knew that was the only way the marriage could last. I always knew that I never wanted to be in an arrangement in my marriage, where we stayed together for reasons other than love. Like for the sake of the kids. And I always told him that.

Maybe, on the other hand, Brooke was telling him she couldn't live without him. And how much she needed him.

I felt like with God's help I could make it on my own. I wasn't afraid of that.

I told him, "The easiest thing in this situation is to just leave the marriage, but sometimes the easiest thing is not the best thing."

He kept saying he knew what he did was wrong but was not willing to separate himself from her.

He insisted that she must stay as his secretary. He was bewitched.

After seeing his determination, I announced that I would call our pastor, which I did. He got so upset with me saying, "As my wife, you are supposed to protect me."

I couldn't believe what I was hearing. *Am I supposed to protect you in your wrongdoing?* I thought.

I explained the situation to the pastor. Eventually, they were both disfellowshipped from the church.

Bill was furious and pulled even further away.

But one day he said, "When she goes on maternity leave, she will not come back."

The pressure was so much to bear, and I could not control my emotions, so I decided to immediately take a couple of weeks off work and travel overseas to stay with one of my girlfriends, whose husband was a pastor.

Bill was aware of my plans, and by February 25, 2010, I was on a plane to Dominica.

Another confession from Bill

While I was away, he phoned me and confessed that Brooke's child was his, adding, "She called me about a week before her husband came back home and said she was pregnant, and it might be mine."

I reminded him that I didn't feel comfortable with her working at the office anymore, even more so knowing that she was pregnant with his child.

Unfortunately, my husband didn't see it that way. He was more concerned about her.

"She didn't get herself pregnant," he said. "All her friends have deserted her. And I want to support her and the baby," he continued.

Wait a minute, what about me? I have two kids for you, I pondered.

He still wanted to be around her, and I just couldn't deal with that.

I asked if her husband knew. He said, "No."

I said, "He needs to know the truth, and if she doesn't tell him, I will." He became very upset. "It is not your place to tell him."

My mind flashed back to my last pregnancy. I realized that God knew why he allowed me to lose that baby a few months back.

I do not know how I would have been able to cope with a young baby while dealing with everything that was now happening.

Thank you, Jesus!

Sometimes in life, things that may seem bad at the time later turn out to be a blessing in disguise. We just need to trust God in everything. The good and the bad.

I had my suspicion for about three years now, but in my heart, I didn't want it to be true. It was a lot for me to take in.

Brooke's husband return

I had left my sons at home, with someone I totally trusted, Onel. While I was away, I learned that Brooke's husband was expected back. This was a very serious matter, and I had no idea how things were going to play out.

I couldn't just stay where I was. I had to protect my sons. I called the airline and moved my flight to an earlier date.

When I did that, Bill accused me of plotting with Brooke's husband to kill him. He started going by his parents to eat.

It was like he was a completely different person than the beautiful soul I married, and I wondered where he was getting these outrageous ideas from.

When Brooke's husband arrived home, she was staying with her now best friend, as I understand it. He had no idea where she was living.

I told Bill he was back, in my own way trying to protect him because despite what he thought, I didn't want him hurt.

Her husband approached Bill, demanding, "Where is my wife?" Bill told him, "I don't know." Not long after that, he saw them in Bill's vehicle, her sitting in front and him driving. This confirmed to him he had been lied to, and it broke his heart even more.

After what Bill did with his wife, he tried to deal with the matter diplomatically.

His first thought, just like mine, had been to save his marriage, and when he finally got to talk to Brooke, he even suggested they move overseas to start a new life together, which she refused.

She later filed for divorce during which her husband asked for a DNA test for her first child. When the results came in, he was not the father; to a son he called his own for five years.

Brooke emptied their bank account and took everything out of their matrimonial home; didn't even leave a spoon, just his clothes.

He lost everything.

After being overseas working four jobs to take care of his family, this was the aftermath.

The fact that neither of them said sorry or showed any remorse exacerbated the situation. I know my situation was bad, but I think his was even worse.

Listening to him tell his story, I felt the pain in his voice. A man broken. My heart ached for him.

Brooke's husband is Bill's cousin, a very good friend of his for many years. Someone he looked up to. What had made the pain worse is that he had confided in Bill about the trouble in their marriage, even about his wife not wanting to be intimate with him.

He expressed to me that his friends were telling him Bill seemed like someone who could murder him and go without a qualm to his funeral.

The time had come round again to submit the VAT for the business, so I went to the office to get information to do it and realized his laptop password was changed. I called him, and he said he would do the VAT himself.

Later, I went to the office and found he'd changed the locks on the door and put on a gate. So, I was locked out. And she was still there.

Eventually, she went on maternity leave.

The birth of their baby in April 2010

I had no idea when the baby was expected, but as God would have orchestrated, it was brought to my attention.

Like many times before, my mom went to our business. He was there, and not too long afterward, one of his friends (Brooke's best friend's husband) came in.

Bill was sitting at his desk with his legs stretched out on another chair. His friend came in very excited, saying that he was uptown when he heard their son was born; he ran all the way to his office.

He gave Bill a high five in all the excitement.

When I heard this, I was amazed because this was a married man. I couldn't believe my ears. *What if his wife were to cheat on him and get pregnant by another man? Would he be that excited?*

It was not a year later that I heard he and his wife were no longer together.

When I found out it was a boy, in my heart I was happy. Call me selfish, but the truth is I didn't want them to have a girl.

However, not very long after that she was back at the office.

Take his child to live with me?

While talking to one of his friends one day, I was telling him that I still wanted to work things out with my husband. He asked me, "Are you willing to take the illegitimate child to live with you?"

I didn't think I could bear it. Honestly, that price was a bit too much to handle.

I heard of some women who, being in the same situation, have done it, but I just didn't think I could have, as much as I wanted the marriage to work.

In fact, one of my friends was in that very situation. Her dad had an affair, but his wife agreed to have her live with them.

We are all different; there are things that others can handle that you just can't and vice versa. We all have our limits.

Bill's family background

We often hear that it is very important to find out about a prospective partner's background before marriage.

Unfortunately, I found out later.

One day my mom called and said that my grandmother phoned her, very upset. Her soul was drowning into the river of her grief because she heard about Bill's family, and she did not like what she heard.

Foreseeing that things were going to end badly, she was feeling sorry for me.

When Bill's mom and I got close, she told me her infidelity story. Bill's dad cheated on her with one of her friends.

Bill was very young at the time, and she went back home to her family overseas.

After a few years and many of her husband's pleas to come back home, however, she returned. Her husband ended his affair, and they committed themselves to each other again. They stayed together until his father died.

His brother also had affairs, and his wife divorced him.

Bill should have thought of how that experience affected his relationship with his dad—how will his action affect his sons?

If your heart is somewhere else, don't marry another because this might come back to haunt you.

Let me give you a bit of advice: don't think that your husband will never cheat on you. Some women say, "My man will never cheat on me because he is getting it real good and plenty from me."

I was not one of those women who thought her husband would never cheat on her. Of course, I didn't want that to happen, but in the back of my mind I knew if he wasn't careful, he would get involved with someone else.

Why do men cheat?

A man doesn't cheat only because he is not happy with his wife. Here are a few reasons why men cheat:

1. *Some men like variety—one woman is not enough. Or they like the thrill of doing something they know is wrong.*

2. *They didn't plan to but allowed their eyes to linger too long on another woman or allowed themselves to be in a compromising position.*

3. *Others were seduced by a persistent woman; he might be able to resist her advances for a while but eventually gives her what she wants. I might be wrong, but I believe this was the case with Bill and Brooke.*

4. *They never truly loved the woman they married; it was all lust, and when the thrill died off or the lady put on a few pounds, they lost interest.*

5. *They cannot control their libido and are sex addicts who want it morning, noon, and night.*

People make mistakes, and that includes spouses as well. Although I didn't want it to happen, I never thought that my husband would never cheat on me.

I do believe that if I had, it would have been a lot harder for me to deal with when he eventually did.

Lessons Learned

1. *Over the years one of my faults has been that I trust too easily. I knew I wouldn't just make up stories and lie to others, and I didn't think others would do that either. It has cost me a lot, but I now realize there are some very deceptive and manipulative people out there, who will do and say almost anything to get what they want, and men are no exception. Looking back, I feel so foolish, falling for Bill's scam, but it taught me a very valuable lesson. As women, we have to be ever so vigilant and exercise great wisdom when we find ourselves in certain situations.*

2. *Never be excited about other people's pain and suffering. You never know what or when yours is going to be.*

3. *Never say never. A lot of women say, "My husband will never cheat!" And live to rue the day.*

CHAPTER 6

Dealing with Loss

Healing doesn't mean the damage never existed.
It means the damage no longer controls our lives.
—*Unknown*

Everyone suffers loss of some sort—loss of a partner, a job, death of a loved one, etc. I am sure that you will agree that these times are the unhappiest moments in our lives.

Bill and I were living together and sleeping in the same bed, but he was being intimate with another woman. Believe it or not, sadly that is the case of a lot more marriages and relationships than we think.

How do they get to that stage? Was that the case from the beginning of the marriage, or did it occur over time? Were there signs that were ignored or never detected?

I think we just need to realize that over time people change.

God spoke to me through dreams

While going through my ordeal, I am convinced, God spoke to me through dreams.

The first such dream I remember was this: *I was on my knees, digging through a dirt tunnel with my bare hands. Bit by bit I caught a glimpse of light. I dug and dug until I made it through to the other side.*

Interpreting it as God showing me, I would be OK, I was comforted.

Another dream I had, I tell below:

My husband and I were relaxing on our bed, just lying there; then I saw Brooke walk right into our bedroom, dressed only in her underwear (her bra and a half slit) and lie down right between us without saying a word.

My heart started to beat faster, and I immediately demanded, "What are you doing here? You must leave now. You have gone too far." While I was protesting, my husband just lay there, mute.

I saw the dream as God informing me of the dynamics between us. I told Bill, and he dismissed it as just a dream, saying I must not make anything of it.

When we were being counseled, he told the counselor this dream and said I was being paranoid over a dream, giving her the impression that it was all just in my head.

He put on a good performance, and the counselor began to believe him. She even said if I wasn't pregnant, she would have prescribed medication for my anxiety.

He liked that and kept mentioning it, trying to convince me that it was all a figment of my imagination. But deep down I knew their friendship was not normal.

On another night I dreamt of someone telling me that one of the employees at our company had something to tell me. The person was called by name, so I knew exactly who it was.

While walking through town the next day I saw him and told him about my dream.

However, he said, "I have nothing to tell."

I was not upset or angry with him. I just reflected that he was properly afraid of saying anything because he didn't want to lose his job.

True enough, after everything was exposed, he confessed to me that Bill had forbidden him to tell me anything.

He also said that when he had been unfaithful to his wife, Bill came and talked to him about it, and he listened.

Now that the shoe was on the other foot, Bill wanted to hear nothing of it.

He even said, "A few times when you passed by the office at lunchtime, she slipped out the back way just as you came in."

I also dreamt I was on my bed, Brooke came inside the room with a little girl and sat on the toilet seat, with the child at her feet.

I asked her, "What are you doing here?"

"I am waiting for Bill," she said.

I ran her out of my bedroom, into the living room and down the stairs. The dream ended with us in the kitchen.

From that moment I just knew the child was his. I saw this as God's way of showing it to me.

What can I do to save my marriage?

Many times, I wondered what I should do or not do to save my marriage. *Why did Bill cheat on me? Had I not gone away to study, would we still be together?*

We had made the decision together and put a plan in place to ensure we were not apart for any extended period, but it had been too much.

Not long after the confession, I contacted a different counselor. Bill agreed to meet with us.

He expressed dissatisfaction that I talked to the pastor. I said I was not comfortable with Brooke. What I really wanted was for him to leave Brooke, but it was clear he was not willing to.

In that meeting she told Bill that sometimes taking some time away from the situation helps people see what is really important. Alas. This, I think, only pushed him further away from me by making him feel comfortable to leave.

I can recall feeling a bit taken aback. I couldn't seem to find a counselor who improved the situation. Just the contrary.

She said I had to decide if I was willing to put aside all the pain and hurt I felt and fight for my marriage. Or just leave the marriage to end.

I told her I wanted to save my marriage. She suggested that I go buy sexy lingerie for later that night. "Are you willing to do this?"

I still loved my husband and was willing to do whatever it took, so I went into town and looked for the sexiest lingerie I could find. Usually, I would be all excited, shopping for lingerie, but this time it was with a heavy heart, wondering if this in itself could make any difference at all.

I finally decided on a red one-piece outfit that left very little to the imagination. *Perfect*, I thought.

That night I showered, put it on, and lay in bed, waiting. Suppressing my emotions, I convinced myself that I needed to at least try.

Hearing him pull into the garage, I quickly threw off the covers, twisted and turned, trying to put myself in the most alluring position, and waited for him to enter the bedroom.

When he opened the door and saw me, he asked, "Weren't you upset with me earlier today, so why do you want to have sex with me now?"

Needless to say, that night we did not have sex. My plan was not good enough to entice him to give himself to me.

Maybe it was because the truth was finally out and he was too ashamed. He probably could not understand why I would still want to be with him after what he had done.

I saw this as a sign that I had lost my husband and Brooke was now the winner in this epic, almost four-years-long love triangle. The fact that he could not give himself to me, as he did so many times before, made things seem final—that he had made up his mind he no longer wanted the marriage.

Actually, *did I really want to have sex with him that night?* He was right. No, this was just a desperate act to try to save my marriage.

I was willing to do anything it took, no matter how hard. At least, if the marriage ended, I could look back and say I tried. I felt good, though, that he was keeping the sex authentic.

My season of deep depression

Feeling unloved and rejected, I went into a deep depression. At times I was so depressed and in such a dark funk that I couldn't even pray.

When going through these difficult times, this is when you need to request prayer from people you know truly care about you, people you trust.

I began to lose a lot of weight because of all the stress; I couldn't eat or sleep.

I reflect, looking back, that my husband confessed the Monday, and I had just returned four days earlier from a business training program in St. Lucia that lasted for just over two weeks. I left, February 2, 2010, and returned on February 18, 2010.

I had always been petite, ever since I knew myself. In fact, when I got married, I weighed only ninety pounds at 5 foot 2 inches.

After having the kids, I did put on some weight but lost most of it.

On that trip I put on about ten pounds because after work I just hung out in my room at the hotel.

I hardly had anything to do, so I slept a lot.

I later saw this as God preparing me in His own way for what was to happen. So, he gave me that time away to fatten me up. Had that not happened, I can't imagine what I would have looked like when I started losing weight. I felt like God was looking out for me. This brought a lot of comfort.

I remember having to literally force myself to eat, and when I did, it was not much. I eventually resembled a figure one.

One of my co-workers said to me one day, "I noticed that you've lost a lot of weight. You should not stress over anyone, but just take care of yourself and your kids."

I don't know for sure if he knew what was going on. As a professional, I kept my work and personal life separate. I had made up my mind in all of this that I would never break down at work, which with God's help I never did. I made sure I cried before or after work.

On more than one occasion when I was at work and had a flood of emotions too much for me to contain, I just quickly went to the bathroom or took a drive somewhere private.

There I cried as much as I needed to, then composed myself, dried my tears and went back to work.

When I got home, I went straight to bed, closed the door, and cried my eyes out. It hurt so much. I felt like a castaway.

It broke me to the core of my soul. I thought no one would ever love me again and asked myself: *Will I ever be able to love again?*

The day I fainted

One day I went to our business office during my lunch hour, as I often did even after Bill's confession. As I opened the door to go up the stairs a disturbing scene greeted me. My husband was standing very close to Brooke, his body touching hers, and whispering something in her ear.

My heart almost jumped out of my chest at the sight. "Why do you have to go so close to her like that?" I asked.

"What do you want now?" he said, in a very forceful and condescending manner.

I froze like a statue. The emotional pressure inside me was off the scales. There was absolutely no sign of remorse from either of them.

Totally distressed, I turned around and began to make my way out of the office. I was so overwhelmed that my body seemed to get weaker and weaker with every step down the stairs. I heard someone call "Delia."

It was a pastor, who just happened to be in the building. I just could not utter the words to respond to him. Mute, I kept slowly going down the stairs, my body getting weaker and weaker with every step. By the time I went through the front door, I could not feel my legs. At that moment I had zero control over my body and began to slowly tumble to the ground.

Thankfully, the pastor was alert and caught me, holding me up for a few minutes until I regained my strength and found my legs again.

If he had not been there, I would have fallen on that hard concrete ground. I could have hit my head and gotten seriously hurt.

This is another time I felt like God was looking out for me. He sent someone right on time when I needed help.

Time for change

That day when I fainted was a wake-up call because from that moment I realized I needed to start taking care of myself.

So, I started to literally force myself to eat, tried to get more sleep, and even took some vitamins to help build my mind and body. Bit by bit my lost weight started coming back, and I was regaining my strength.

They cared nothing about me. Far from it. They were going around together, enjoying themselves. I had to accept the simple fact that my husband chose my best friend over me, our family, and all we had together.

He chose her, and there was nothing I could do about it. That was clear. By necessity, I decided to let go of the situation, shifting my focus to my kids, who at the time were nine and two. I knew that as their mother I needed to be there to take care of them.

That is when I took responsibility for my own happiness and began to indulge in some self-love by buying myself new dresses, having my hair done, going out with friends, and having a good time.

I began to love having my pictures taken, and everywhere we went I would have my kids or friends take my photo. This was a new hobby. Of course, after a while they all got fed up and started to protest, but that did not stop me. I just started taking selfies. Where there is a will there is a way. Don't laugh.

I thought about my two sons, knowing if I continued withdrawing from life like this, I might not be around to take care of them. The stress might cause a mental breakdown, or I might unintentionally do something to hurt myself. As their mother, I wanted to be there for them in every possible way.

I heard of many cases where stepmothers or stepfathers mistreated or abused their step kids. No way did I want mine to be in that position.

So, I began to take my focus off my loss and started to think about myself and my sons.

The day Bill left home

Bill stopped eating at home, as I mentioned. I would cook and leave his food only to come back and see it untouched. When I asked why, he explained, "I ate with my mom."

I told his mom, and her reply was, "He said he's afraid to eat at home because he thinks you want to kill him" and asked, "Do you want me to die?" So, they allowed him to stay.

Not only did he stop eating at home, but he also started to sleep out as well. Sometimes I would lie in bed, waiting for Bill to come home, but he never did.

On April 19, 2010, again he did not return home, and he has not slept at home since. I called him and pleaded, "Can you please come home and let us try and work things out together?" But he wouldn't budge.

Every night I had to face that lonely bed. Sleeping alone, nobody to cuddle up tight with and throw my leg over. The bed that was once filled with love and comfort and great pleasure was now empty and void like the conditions existing before God created the earth.

I went to his parents on April 29, 2010, and asked them to ask him for me.

On May 1, 2010, which was my first son's birthday, his mother told me he said he was not coming back home.

I could not ruin my son's birthday, so I withheld this terrible news, trying to act as normal as possible, hiding away all the pain.

Not long after that, he told me himself he needed some time to think and was going to stay with his parents for a while. I still called him. On May 9, 2010—a week after the birth of their son—he told me "I fasted and prayed, and God told me to leave my family."

I was very much astonished because I knew the God I served would be in favor of families staying together, not break them apart. I remembered what 2 Thessalonians 2:11: "And for this cause God shall send them strong delusion, that they should believe a lie."

This is what happens when people choose to stay in sin and do their own thing. At that point, I knew no doubt he was under the control of the devil.

In that same conversation he said, "All my life I have been thinking about other people, but now I am going to think about myself." Those words had a lot of weight to them. He was on a path that seemed not to include me.

I went to talk to one of our leading pastors, a good friend of my husband. I can never forget what he said to me on that day: "Your husband is demon possessed. I can't tell you to end your marriage, but both of them came to me for advice and Brooke said that she loved and wanted your husband."

Basically, in a roundabout way, he was telling me my marriage was over, a fact I was reluctant to accept even after Bill confessed to the affair.

What was I holding on to? Was I delusional?

Onel, a supporting friend

Word went around the neighbourhood about Bill and Brooke. In fact, the news spread like wildfire around the whole country. That's what happens when you live in a small nation of about 120,000 people.

Bill was popular all over the country. News of the affair spread through the village, then through the over twenty churches in our denomination scattered in different parts of the country. Then into those villages. Yes, these people told people overseas as well.

When you are going through your worst is when you find out who your true friends are. At this point I received support from church members.

Anyone who told Bill he was wrong or associated with me immediately became his enemies, even his own relatives. Of course, some people chose to believe what Bill was saying to them and kept their distance from me.

Fortunately for me, one of the persons who supported me was willing to go above and beyond just uttering words of comfort. She wasn't happy about what happened, so she decided to stick around to help.

Let me introduce you to my friend Onel. A young person but very mature, she was the babysitter for our second son. Her support would prove to be critical to my survival.

When I was unable to cope, she was there, helping to look after the boys, feeding them, helping with homework, and in the evening helping me clean, cook, etc.

This she did out of her kind heart, not looking for payment. At one point she even moved in with me.

She had first-hand experience of exactly what I was going through. I asked her what it was like for her. "Many times, I thought that you would go crazy," she told me.

One day while we were driving home, Onel was in the front passenger seat, and my second son in the backseat. Unwittingly, I drove the vehicle into a fence.

Terrified, she screamed out loudly, "What are you doing?"

To her it was like I was in a different world.

But hearing her voice, I sprang out of my daze, immediately pulling away from the fence, and steered us back on the road before any great damage was done.

Only God alone knows what would have happened if she had not been in the vehicle that day.

One of the things that put me in an even more depressed mode was when people would phone and tell me things about Bill and Brooke. Where they met them and what they were doing together.

On one occasion a friend told me that Brooke was moving into the house. Noticing how depressed that made me, Onel called my friend and told her not to tell me what Bill was doing because it was breaking me down.

Another time, she remembered, when our younger son was at the hospital, Bill did not even come to visit. Instead, he sent his mother.

She also recalled that my younger son would keep saying, "I want my daddy. Where is my daddy?"

She acted like my guardian angel. Doing what she could to help me.

Strangely enough, she admitted to me that when we first met, I looked so uptight and unfriendly, but as she got to know me better, she saw I was so nice.

She remembered when Bill moved out to live with his parents. From time to time, he just came to the house and started arguing.

Bill accusing me of cheating

It got back to me that Bill was spreading the rumor that I cheated on him. So, every time I saw Bill talking to someone, an intense feeling of unease and worry gripped me.

Not knowing what lies he was telling, I would go and talk to them as well.

After a while, this began to negatively affect my mental health, so I decided to stop. I remember saying to myself: *I know the truth and God knows the truth and that is all that really matters.*

Before Bill moved out, I remember, we were in the dining area, sitting at the table, talking. I asked him, "When are you going to stop going around and spreading lies about me?"

He didn't try to defend himself by saying, "I am not lying."

His response was, "Do you want people to only think bad of me?"

Not till then did I truly understand that he was trying to ruin my reputation. It was all a plan to take the focus off him and make me look bad in people's eyes.

Feeling let down by God

All my life I have tried to live a good Christian life. I want to make it to heaven, and in order for me to do that I had to be faithful to God.

One thing I was very proud of myself with was that I was faithful in my marriage and never cheated on Bill. Cheating on him meant that I would also be unfaithful to God, which I did not want to do.

I am someone who has always been content with what is mine, which included my husband. I never looked at another man in any romantic way, never kissed or even held another man's hand.

To hear rumors going around, accusing me of something I didn't do, was a blow to the heart.

I saw it as a spiritual attack, where Satan was trying to degrade and debase me in a way I didn't deserve.

Many times, I asked God, *"When are you going to vindicate me?"*

To me God was just too slow in coming to my defence.

Despite this, I remained faithful to Him.

Words of comfort from my nine-year-old son

One evening while I was lying down in my bed in tears, my son came and sat next to me.

He took my Bible from the dresser, gave it to me, and told me to turn to Romans 8:28, which says, "And we know that all things work together for God to them that love

God, to them who are called according to his purpose." I read it, then put the Bible down.

He took the Bible up again and told me to turn to Philippians 4:13, which says, "I can do all things through Christ who strengthens me." After reading, I put the Bible down again.

He told me to take up the Bible and turn to Job 23:10: "But he knoweth the way that I take; when he hath tried me, I shall come forth as gold."

At that moment I felt like God himself was talking to me, through my son. These texts were pitch perfect.

Another time I picked up my quarterly (a weekly Bible study by Seventh Day Adventists) and started turning the pages to find the lesson for the week.

That quarter the study was called "Emotions," and I was naming aloud the different emotions: stress, guilt, resilience. Then I came to the study of the week, jealousy.

My older son, sitting next to me, as soon as he heard the word "jealousy," said, "Don't you know that she was jealous of you—that's why she did what she did?"

I don't think he really understood what he was saying. *How could he, at only nine years old?*

One of my friends expressed similar sentiments. She said that Brooke saw me writing checks—was jealous and wanted to do the same.

On more than one occasion, in Brooke's presence I wrote routine checks whether to pay for fuel, groceries, etc. I had no idea that in her mind she was envious of that.

How disgusting, I thought, that another woman's lust for a lifestyle upgrade was worth the devastation of my family.

The day my first son cried and the impact on the kids

In any broken relationship the kids tend to suffer the most. Without their doing anything wrong, their lives are turned upside down—all due to decisions made by their parents in which they have no say.

They are the spectators in the match between the mom and dad, both whom they love so much. Sadly, sometimes they are forced to choose sides.

Our boys' happiness was being negatively impacted as well.

Many parents fail to realize this because all their focus might be on trying to get through the ordeal themselves.

I knew my first son must be sad and tried to get him to talk about how what was happening was affecting him, but he always said, "I'm OK."

He never showed any emotion about the matter. I even arranged some school counseling for him. Maybe he would open up to someone else. But that process did not seem to change anything.

Until one day I was at our new home, sitting outside in the yard, going through his schoolwork. In one of his books was an essay he had written.

In it he confessed to telling his grandmother all his problems. *What problems?* I thought immediately. *What's he talking about?*

So, I showed him the essay and asked. I reassured him that he could tell me anything, that I wanted to help. His eyes welled up, and he began to sob uncontrollably.

In spite of everything that was happening in our lives, I had never seen him express any emotions until now. *Had he been trying to be strong for me?* I don't know.

He cried for a long time, moving around, unable to stand still, as though he was seeking a place of refuge.

He went from the yard to the porch, to the living room inside the house, then his bedroom. This he did while still sobbing. I was there, following behind him every step of the way, trying to console him.

As I looked at my son's tear-stained face, with puffy eyes and snot running out his nose, I felt a tightness in my chest and the air like razor blades moving through my heart. I could not bear to see his pain.

It took everything in me to battle the emotions raging inside me. Knowing I had to be strong for him, I tried my very best not to break down and weep. Nothing I did or said could have soothed him.

Not knowing what else to do, I decided to call a counselor. He took the phone from me and listened while still quietly sobbing. I don't know what was said, but it helped.

Not until then did my son's emotional turmoil calm down and the waves crawl gently to the shore.

In a way I thought this experience might have been a good one because maybe the tears might help release the pain he was holding inside for so long.

Tears are a language that God understands.

That was the first and last time my son showed such emotions.

My older son, though young, was very observant. He paid attention to what was happening around him and without being prompted would tell me what he saw. One day as soon as he came back from a visit with his dad, he said to me, "Mom, Jason started to call Dad, Dad." Jason was Brooke's first son. To him that was perplexing because he was used all these years to hearing Jason calling his dad "Uncle Bill."

Another time after coming from his dad's office, he said to me that there was a note on the fridge, saying to refill the water bottles, signed "by management," at the end, but Brooke had added her name next to "management."

I simply smiled.

The grieving process

Many times, I felt like a high-suction power vacuum cleaner had literally sucked all of the energy from my body; I just wanted to stay in bed.

I remember one day while lying in my bed, feeling very depressed, I heard my phone ring.

"Hello," I picked up and said. An unknown female voice on the other end identified herself as a counselor in one of our churches. As I told her what I was experiencing, she said, "You are grieving the loss of your husband and best friend."

She was able to give a name to what I'd been going through for so many months.

To that point in my mind, grief was only associated with death. Never did I hear that someone whose husband had left her was grieving the loss of her husband.

This was a new concept for me, but it then became clear that I was indeed grieving the loss of not only my husband but my best friend as well. It was a double whammy, losing two people who were very close to me and an important part in my life.

That was indeed a lot for one person to bear.

I heard that divorce is a unique type of loss, comparable to a death. Even though both are still alive, the other party will no longer be in your life as in the past. That's why the emotional stages of divorce are very similar to those of grief after a death or trauma.

Symptoms of grief can be emotional, physical, social, or religious in nature.

In general, getting over a loss of a spouse through infidelity or otherwise follows the usual seven stages of grief. If you experienced this before or are experiencing it now, I want you to tick off the stages as they apply to you. *Is this what you went through? Are going through?* Everyone grieves differently, so honor your own experience at your pace.

It is very important to identify where you are in this process. You can always come back to this list at any point to update. The best thing you can do is to let the process take its course.

- [ ] Shock—Is my marriage really over? Did my husband leave me for someone else? You think back to your wedding vows when you both said the words, "till death do us part." The feeling of shock starts affecting you physically. Now here you are: you can't eat, you can't sleep, you start losing weight.

- [ ] Denial—This can't be happening. Maybe we can work things out. Maybe if I change this or that about myself and do everything he wants me to, he will change his mind and come back.

- [ ] Anger—Why is this happening to me? I don't deserve it. I did my part, I was faithful. I did everything for this man: cooked his food, washed and ironed his clothes, and supported him in every way I knew how. Why did he do this to me?

- [ ] Bargaining—You try to forget about what your partner did. You convince yourself that no one else could love you the way he did. Then try to convince your partner that maybe it's not too late—that the relationship can be saved.

- [ ] Guilt—Was it all my fault? Maybe if I hadn't done or said so-and-so, he'd not have left. I did not do enough to save my relationship. I should have done this or that.

- ☐ Depression—Deep sadness and loneliness start to kick in as you begin to really understand the magnitude of your loss. You begin to think about how your life has changed as a result of the loss of your partner, e.g., in your finances, etc. You might find yourself wanting to always be alone, not around your friends and family. Or you just want to be a couch potato—lying down on the couch or in bed, doing nothing, feeling like you have absolutely no energy to do anything.

- ☐ Acceptance—This is the final stage of the grieving process. You will start to find it easier to talk about your loss without it having a great impact on you. Finally, be able to say his name without breaking down. Even though you might still be feeling sadness, you accept the loss. You now begin to think and plan your future and ways to move on with your life.

The grieving process can feel like an emotional roller coaster, but coming to terms with what happened is integral to healing. Rather than suppressing your emotions, work through them.

If you find yourself unable to cope, it is very important to talk to someone. Get well-trained professional help if you need to. There is no shame in getting help. This can prove very beneficial in maintaining your sanity and even saving your life.

The dark side of infidelity and betrayal

When facing rejection from your partner, especially after building a life together for years, it "hurts like hell."

We are all different, and a lot of us deal with rejection differently.

I heard of a lady who suspected her husband was having an affair. We will call her Julie. Julie noticed a change in her husband. He kept his cell phone on him at all times. Before, he just threw it down anywhere. One morning, seeing his phone on the table, she started searching through it. One of the messages read, "Hey, babe, I really wanted you last night."

Coming out of the shower, he saw the phone conspicuously lying in her hand.

"What should I make of this message?" she asked.

As she proceeded to go out to the backyard, her knees got weak; they started trembling, and she collapsed at the front door. He just stood at the doorway and did nothing while the baby was screaming, "waah, waah" repetitively.

Trying to get up, she was only able to stand on her third try. That same morning, she was scheduled to start her small business from home. Despite what she was going through, she decided to still go ahead.

However, she fell into a deep depression and couldn't sleep; her appetite was affected, and like me she lost a lot of weight. Her husband kept denying he was cheating.

Next, she went into detective mode, questioning people as to whether they had seen them together. One of the things that helped her not go over the edge was speaking about it to loved ones and close friends.

He finally admitted that he was in love with another woman and, raising his voice, said, "I do not love you anymore!"

As her ears heard these cruel words, her world closed in on her.

He was sitting with his back turned to the kitchen. A voice said to her, "Get up and take the knife and stab him in his head." She knew that was the devil speaking and didn't move because God was working with her at her lowest point.

Instead, she just sat there, speaking the language of tears uncontrollably for a while. Then she got up, went to the restroom and washed her face.

And had it not been for her faith in God, she would have committed murder and suicide.

That night she felt she couldn't sleep and at the same time couldn't stay awake because the pain was so much to bear.

He sat there quietly, in silence. In that moment she heard the Holy Spirit speak, saying, "When you are at your lowest, praise God."

"How can I praise you when I don't feel like it?" she replied.

However, obeying, she went to lie down on the bed and started praising God. It felt so awkward. It was like she had just been knocked out and fallen into a deep sleep. The next thing she knew, it was morning and she was awake, not feeling as bad as the night before.

Without her saying anything, a family friend came to the house that day and spent the day with her. Her friend had no idea she was suicidal.

Cricket was on TV—twelve runs needed from two balls. *Impossible*, she thought.

The first ball hit for a six, and so did the second.

She used this as a lesson, telling herself: *"Look at that when a thing seems impossible to me, with God it is possible."* From that day on, through the Holy Spirit she began to feel increasingly stronger. He took away the hurt.

Every day as well the romantic feeling was eroding, disappearing bit by bit, until she started looking on him as a brother.

While enduring her ordeal, Julie was still able to care for their three young children. But she hadn't been prepared for the end, so it knocked her very hard when he finally left her.

She recalled lying in bed at nights, contemplating ways to rid this woman from the face of the earth—such as putting dynamite under her house.

Thank God, she never followed through.

Her friends came by, praying and fasting with her, which really helped. Attending an early-morning prayer meeting every Wednesday in church also helped. With all this support, she stayed strong and moved on with her life.

Looking at her story, I see differences but also so many similarities in our situation.

These difficult times can prove that *"You are braver than you believe, stronger than you seem, smarter than you think, and loved more than you know."*

A. A. Milne

On the other hand, if you allow them, they can bring out the devil in you.

We hear many stories in the news of how a spouse or partner reacted to infidelity. As I mentioned before, people deal with things differently, and the truth is no one knows exactly how they will react and what they will do until they are in the situation. Some women end up committing homicide, suicide, and physical assault. While for others the pressure is too much; they have a mental breakdown.

I have heard of women even resorting to sexual assault. The anger and rage are so much that they chop off their man's penis. Another not only chopped it off but cooked it with noodles.

Lorena Bobbitt, from Virginia, was the first to make headlines around the world when she cut off her husband's penis on June 23, 1993. This she did with a kitchen knife, then drove away with it in her car, and threw it in a field.

How can you prevent yourself from taking the dark path?

For me, thank God, I never had any thoughts of hurting myself, Bill, or Brooke. I have never been a violent person. I don't even know how to curse someone just to be hurtful. That is so foreign to me.

For others, this might not be the case; it might take great effort and self-constraint to prevent themselves from causing harm to themselves or others.

Violence is never the answer unless done to protect oneself or those you love from being physically hurt. It greatly disrupts your life and the lives of those around you. Most times, you end up losing your freedom by going to jail. Being away from your children, family, and friends is not an easy price to pay.

Use the list below (author unknown) to help you get through these dark moments:

12 Daily Reminders

1. *The past cannot be changed.*
2. *Things will get better with time.*
3. *Opinions don't define your reality.*
4. *Everyone's journey is different.*
5. *Judgments are a confession of character.*
6. *Overthinking will lead to sadness.*
7. *Happiness is found within.*
8. *Positive thoughts create positive things.*
9. *Smiles are contagious.*

10. Kindness is free.

11. You only fail if you quit.

12. What goes around comes around.

Lessons learned

1. At times in life, it helps to just take a step back and assess what is most important and take it from there.

2. If a man really wants to leave you, he will no matter what you do, even if you try to change who you are as a person to please him. So be true to you.

3. Always remember that God is one person who, I know for sure, will never leave you. So, you are never alone.

4. Have someone to confide in, someone you trust, when going through challenging situations. I spoke to friends and family and where necessary sought counseling.

5. Be thankful for the little blessings in life, not just the big ones.

CHAPTER 7

My Turning Point

Every test in our life makes us BITTER or BETTER.
Every problem comes to BREAK US or MAKE US.
The choice is ours whether we become VICTIM or VICTOR.
—Unknown

On the morning of May 11, 2010, two days after Bill said he was not coming back home, I went downstairs to prepare breakfast to start my day. Upon approaching the dining room, I froze at the sight of a window leaning on the wall below the window frame. It was not broken or damaged in any way.

Very scared and not wanting to go any further by myself, I shouted to Onel, who was upstairs. She immediately ran down, and we proceeded into the dining room. Onel said, "I heard the neighbours dogs barking last night."

During the night I'd heard a noise myself but didn't take it for anything.

Nothing was missing from the house. Everything was still intact; the fridge, stove, TV, etc., were all there.

I found the whole thing very unusual. There was no indication that the window had simply fallen down.

I reported the matter to the police. However, seeing that nothing was missing, there wasn't much they could do.

I called someone to fit the window back in and fix it. *It must have been Bill*, I thought, *trying to scare me out of our home. He knew that window was unsteady.*

When I spoke to my mom, she said Bill had spoken to her, describing exactly how to take the window out and put it back in.

This just confirmed my suspicions. He was the one who did it. However, no other "break-in" followed.

Financial difficulties

Even making over $6,000 a month, I was left virtually penniless. As well as the business loan, the home mortgage was deducted from my salary, at over $2,600, plus taxes and other statutory payments were deducted. Regardless of my financial problems, I always tithed. A grand total of about $200 remained.

The arrangement we had was that I would pay the mortgage, and the profits from the business paid for the house bills and reinvestment in the business.

There was no court order in place, stipulating what he should give, so now he gave what he pleased, which was irregular and insufficient. I told him my predicament, reminding him how high the bills were. But he didn't offer a cent more.

Trying to manage everything on my own, I felt overwhelmed. Bill was no longer around to help with breakfast. Also, I hadn't experienced money worries for years. I began resenting my current financial position.

It became even more difficult when the kids entered a new grade in school. I reached the point where it took credit cards to buy school uniforms and books. I had to find means and ways to cut my expenses.

At times I took public transport, not being able to afford to buy fuel.

To help cut costs, I decided to transfer my younger son from his private preschool to a cheaper school.

However, when I told the school owner, out of the goodness of her heart she told me not to move him: "You can pay half of the fees instead from now on." I gladly accepted. Such kindness in time of need will never be forgotten.

Choosing a lawyer

If ever you find yourself in need of legal services, please ensure you take time to choose the right lawyer. Sad to say, some lawyers are only in it for the money and do not have any genuine interest in your situation. Don't just choose based on popularity, which was my mistake. I tried contacting a former schoolmate of mine, who was now a lawyer, but never got her.

So, when someone suggested a well-known lawyer, I took her advice.

On, May 12, 2010, at our appointment, I told her my situation. She advised that to do anything legally, she would first have to file in the courthouse.

I had a choice, the lawyer told me, between legal separation—by which we would remain married but live apart following a court order—or divorce.

I never believed in divorce; in my mind, when God instituted marriage, it was meant to be forever. However, being financially in turmoil and desperately needing help, I reluctantly had the lawyer file a separation petition on the grounds of infidelity. In fact, I still had a bit of hope that Bill might return to me. I had it bad, didn't I? Or maybe I was just foolish.

My lawyer explained that with that choice, neither he nor I could remarry. But remarrying was the last thing on my mind. The aim was to put myself in a financial position where I could pay my bills.

Now, the problem was, where was I going to find the $3,500 to pay the lawyer's fees? I still had the business check book, so I naively wrote a check and went to the bank to take out some money. I should have anticipated what I found when I got there. My name had been taken off the account; the bank could no longer honor any withdrawal with my signature. He hadn't told me a thing, of course.

What do I do now?

The lawyer made it clear that she would not be starting anything before payment. The business had online banking, so I decided to go online, transfer the money from the business account to our personal account, then take the cash from there.

This, I was able to do successfully. So, I got the money and handed it over to my lawyer.

Ladies, do take this bit of advice. When you are going to court, make sure that your hair is well done and you look good.

That is exactly what I did. I dressed to impress. When I stepped out in the court, he'd be bound to notice me.

Don't go there looking like a grandma or like you are nobody's child. Let him look at you and see what he is missing. Some husbands regret their decision to leave their wife but would never admit it because of pride.

I remember one time when I was entering the courtroom, Bill went and opened the door for me. I was gobsmacked. This was something he had not done for years. The judge, observing the scene, commented, "Look, he is even opening the door for her."

Till now I don't know what to make of that. I guess life is full of surprises.

My mother's advice

If I had followed my mother's advice from a few years prior, I don't think I would have been in such a dire financial situation. Turning to me one day, Mom had said, "I don't know why, but the spirit moved me to tell you to move some money from the joint account and put it aside in your son's name."

She had been pondering for two weeks, wondering how to tell me this because she knew how much I loved Bill and how committed I was to him. She just did not know how I would react.

I became very upset with her. "Shame on you, Mommy, I never expected you to encourage me in doing wrong. As Christians, we are not supposed to hide things from our husband," I said naively.

She later confessed to me that in that moment she felt so bad, knowing to herself she didn't do anything wrong.

I am so sorry, Mom, I never meant to hurt you.

This happened a couple years before our marriage broke down. If I had listened to her, how much better my position would have been financially.

Bill's disruptive visits

Although Bill was living away from home, he kept coming back and taking out his stuff bit by bit. This was mentally taunting to me—as if he were stabbing a wound in the same spot just to cause more pain.

Whenever I felt like I was beginning to accept the situation, there he'd be at the door, just showing up, and he did this mostly when I was leaving for work.

On one occasion when Bill came to the house, I was just getting into the car. He went upstairs, calling me to unlock the bedroom door; we normally locked it for extra security just in case of a break-in. I asked, "What about your key?" He said he didn't have it. Suddenly I heard one big bang.

Upstairs, the bedroom door was now open—with a big hole next to the knob. And the frame by the lock was shattered.

Staying with me at the time, my brother went to see what was going on. When Bill saw him there, he said threateningly, "They will have to scrape up your splattered body from the floor if you so much as try to do anything to me."

I took pictures of the door to my lawyer, expressing concern for my safety, seeing that he was now showing signs of aggression.

I told her I wanted to get a restraining order, to which she replied that the law states that he would have to physically hurt me before I could get one.

I could not believe what I was hearing.

"This cannot be right," I protested.

Another time he came to the house and said he was there to cut the boys' hair. The boys were next door at their cousins'. So, I went to get them.

Then deciding I didn't want to be around him, I left for a drive.

The next day, he dropped by, accusing me of abandoning my kids. He accosted me: "Do you call yourself a good mother?"

"Well, you are the best father in the world," I replied in a tone dripping with sarcasm.

The emotional and psychological trauma caused by him just dropping in unannounced every so often to take this and take that was alarming. Sometimes—declaring, "This is still my house"—he seemed bent on causing argument and confusion.

It made it harder for me to cope. Also, it was unhealthy for the kids. I became so frustrated that one day I packed a suitcase with his clothes and threw it out the window. This infuriated him.

What made matters worse for me was that from home I could see Brooke's vehicle every Saturday at lunchtime after church, parked in his parents' yard; I had a perfect view; it was a stone's throw away. Although Bill and Brooke were disfellowshipped, they still went to church.

After a while, with all the intermittent disruptions and reminders, I felt like I would go mad. So, I decided to leave the house.

This, I did in an attempt to protect my mental health.

To me, my sanity was worth much more than the house or any material thing.

I remember some people questioning me. They couldn't understand why I just vacated the house, leaving it for Bill and Brooke to move in.

I took very minimal household items with me.

He moved back into the house, of course, and she started to hang out there.

I realized that because I could not afford to buy new stuff, I needed to go back for some necessary items, the washing machine and the fridge. Besides, I had to look after not just my needs but the kids' needs as well.

However, when I put the key into the lock and turned it, the door was not opening. Bill had changed the lock.

What do I do now?

I could not call and tell him why I was there. He would definitely not agree to it.

Something told me to go to the back of the house. Fortunately for me there were some blocks stacked up, so I climbed on top up to the veranda. Luckily, I was able to get into the house through an open window. I unlocked the door from the inside and got the stuff out with the help of family members.

Loss of my job

I remember sitting in my boss's office one day; he was inquiring into a problem with the accounts. I explained that it was only a simple matter and had already been sorted.

Immediately, he started fidgeting in his chair, his eyes flicking from side to side as if searching for an escape. His words no longer quite coming together in full sentences.

To try to help to calm him, I said, "It's OK."

"I thought the situation was much worse," he finally uttered.

I could think of no reason for such odd behavior until I received my dismissal letter.

He realized while talking to me that he'd reported something completely different to the head office and knew it had resulted in the decision to fire me. And that it was too late to stop what he had unwittingly already set in motion.

This was truly a dire situation. I remember, when I received the letter, I talked to God in my mind, replaying the scenario: "Lord I have lost my marriage and now my job. Please don't let me lose my kids."

That was my biggest fear. They were all I had left.

I felt like I was going through the Job period of testing found in Job 1:13-19 when he lost his livestock, servants, and ten children who all died in one day due to marauding invaders or natural catastrophes.

I was a single woman on my own, with no other help financially. As a matter of fact, coming from a poor family, I had no one at all to help me.

I had no savings.

Where was I going to get the bare minimum of money to survive and pay rent, buy food, fuel, etc. for me and my boys?

However, one positive thing came out of this experience; that it dissolved the salary assignment with the bank. You see, yet again what the devil intended for bad, God had used for my good.

Whenever I am going through difficulties, I always look for the silver lining and take time to be thankful to God for it.

On Facebook one day, I saw this quotation posted by "Lessons taught by life." It read: *"If you focus on the hurt, you will continue to suffer. If you focus on the lesson, you will continue to grow."*

I started straightaway to seek another job. About three months later, a friend told me about an opening. So, I sent in my application and was invited for an interview. Offered the job, I gladly accepted, even at a salary of $2,000 a month less than what I was getting at my last job.

I have learned in life that you have to take what you get until you can get what you want. A little is better than nothing at all.

When I started to work, the bank sent documents for me to assign my salary to the loan again, but I never did. I could not because that would have put me in an even worse financial situation.

Moving back home

When the judge heard that I lost my job, in a court session she said, "You will have to move back in the matrimonial home." Chilling words. I remembered the reason why I left the house in the first place: to protect my psyche.

I was reluctant to move back in with Bill still living there and people telling me Brooke was always at the house.

"Bill is living there," I told the judge. Before she could respond, maybe fearing being told that he had to move out, Bill convinced the judge, "The house is big enough for both of us."

I was shaking in my shoes every time I thought of my fate, but my back was against the wall.

Bill later told me, "You don't need to bring any appliances to the house because I have everything."

One of my schoolmates, Donna, was visiting from America. We had not seen each other for years. When I told her how hard it had been for me, she volunteered to go to the house with me.

On our way she asked about Brooke's husband and said, "Wouldn't it be something if you and her husband were to get together?"

Then she told me that the same thing happened to Shania Twain: her best friend had an affair with her husband. But Shania ended up marrying the best friend's husband.

"Being with someone else is the last thing on my mind," I announced.

I started believing that all men are the same and convinced myself that I was better off alone. I just abruptly or even rudely at times dismissed advances, fearful of trusting the wrong one.

To protect myself, I avoided dating and having close relationships with the opposite sex for years.

I recall one day while I was lying in bed, my phone rang. "Hello," I answered.

I heard an unknown male voice on the other end of the line. He started expressing his desire to go out with me and asked if I had a boyfriend. "Yes, God is my man," I told him and just put the phone back on its base. Don't judge me. I was in a bad place.

Anyway, when we arrived, Bill had stacked the living-room sofas one on top of the other, so there was nowhere to sit except for the cold tile floor.

Instead of angrily confronting him, Donna suggested taking a sheet to cover them to show him I was supporting him.

I did just that.

I felt the need to have a prayer session and the house anointed before moving back in. So, I invited an elder, a well-known prayer warrior in my former church, to come lead us in this. We prayed as he went around the house, putting anointing oil on the doors and on different items.

I did not tell Bill.

However, he found out about it because the oil stained his bedroom door. He was not pleased. He eventually changed the door.

The boys and I moved back in, and seeing the chairs stacked up, they asked me, "Why are the chairs packed away? Where will we sit?" I told them their father packed them away, when watching TV, they would have to sit on the floor.

I didn't say anything to Bill concerning it.

But a few days later we were in the bedroom and heard chairs moving around in the living room. The boys went outside and came back running. "Daddy is putting down the chairs," they told me—their faces lit up with excitement.

There was a clock with both Bill's and my name on it. It was made of wood in the shape of our home country of St. Vincent. It was one of our wedding gifts.

As I looked at it, I noticed someone had removed my name.

However, if you went close enough, you could still faintly see my name. It was not as pronounced as Bill's.

I just smiled to myself. I saw it as her way of putting me out of the picture.

Bill used to leave his vehicle with Brooke on Fridays, and she would come right in the yard to pick him up for church on Saturdays.

He started taking our kids to her house, which did not make me happy. I protested, but there was nothing else I could think of to do about it.

You have been served

One day my lawyer called. "I received some documents from your husband's lawyer," she informed me and invited me to her office to discuss the options.

Bill had filed for divorce. He didn't just want a separation but wanted to end the marriage. It was a complete shock to me! I was not even aware that more than one petition could be filed in court at the same time. That just shows how much I knew about the court system: very little.

Having been married for twelve years, at the age of thirty-three I found myself at this crossroad. It is not necessarily the norm for the husband to leave the wife for the mistress, but in my case it was. I could not help but think that she pressured him to do so.

I read through the documents in my lawyer's office, tears flowing down my face, seeing the lies he had put there. He testified:

1. For the last two years we were not together but made an arrangement to stay together for the sake of the kids.

2. He did not know what I did with my salary because I was not spending it on the home.

3. We had irreconcilable differences.

I could understand why he would say number three, but the other two were just lies. My mind went back to when he told the court that we never took out a loan for the business. Luckily, I had documents from the bank to prove otherwise which I filed. Strikingly, he did not include infidelity despite the fact that he was spreading rumors saying I cheated. Proving he did not believe his own lie.

Looking penetratingly at me, my lawyer said, "In my many years in legal work I have never seen anyone so angry. You must have done something to Bill for him to be so upset."

Are my ears failing me? I could not believe what I was hearing. It felt like a very low blow. I was already knocked down and deeply distressed by what I was reading—and now to hear my lawyer say that. *How could she represent me effectively, seeing the divorce as all my fault?* But I was stuck with her; I had no funds to go elsewhere.

If you think that was bad, wait until you hear what happened next.

Failing to advise me of the pros and cons, she told me that I had to decide if I was going to pursue my application (changing it to a divorce) or his. Adding that if I chose his, mine will be added to it in the court documents as well. I decided I might as well go with his.

As soon as I communicated that decision, she fired back: "This is a new case. So, before I do anything else, you will have to pay me another $3,500."

This proved to me that she was only in it for the money. She could have told me that before I made my decision.

I had no idea where I was going to get that money from, with no savings and living from paycheck to paycheck.

As God would orchestrate it, my lawyer called me one day and said she received a check from Bill. This was when I had lost my job and been told to move back into the matrimonial house.

I think he figured if he gave me a check, I might not move back in. He might have interpreted it as an advance on my share of the marital property.

The check was for $10,000, but my lawyer informed me that she was taking out her fees, so I only saw $6,000 of it. I knew she took more money than she should have, but I just decided to leave it be.

Looking at my rent and other monthly expenses I realized that this money would not last long and decided to move back "home."

Before granting the divorce, the judge sent Bill and me to a mediator. I guess to give us one last chance to work things out. Bill was not keen on it but went anyway. In that meeting he boldly declared, "me nah turn back now," a popular political slogan.

Disappointed yet again with my lawyer, I was left speechless in court when the judge asked what she should put as the grounds for divorce. This was when my lawyer was informing me that I had to choose one of Bill's reasons in his petition. I wished she had said that to me before to be more prepared.

With this information, I would have decided to continue with my petition instead of his.

I knew none of those was the real cause for the breakdown in the marriage, which was infidelity on his part. Now I had to choose. After deliberating with myself, I chose number three: irreconcilable differences.

After the divorce, we had to go back to court. While entering the courtroom, I could hear the judge talking to the lawyers already there. I caught part of the sentence, "should not have given the divorce and they have two young children."

They must be talking about us, I said to myself.

Does infidelity always have to lead to divorce?

Infidelity does not always have to lead to divorce. If you are currently experiencing it, all might not be lost. There could still be hope yet.

One of the main problems is when one person wants the marriage and the other one does not.

Some couples love each other enough and decide to stay together. They try to work things out by maybe getting counseling. A lot of times, men refuse to go but are more prone to the idea after being unfaithful if they are serious about reconciliation.

Most times, rebuilding the relation begins with a *Real Apology*:

1. *Freely Admitting Fault*

2. *Fully Accepting Responsibility*

3. *Humbly Asking for Forgiveness*

4. *Immediately Changing Behavior*

5. *Actively Rebuilding Trust*

At the end of the day, if the person really cares about you, he will fight for you not only when it is convenient but also when it is difficult and messy and aches all over.

Let us not forget that the reconciliation process is not easy, but that does not mean that you can't give it a try.

I learnt a very important lesson that has stuck with me even to this day.

It is better to stay quiet when angry because you might just say something that you will regret. I so regret those words I uttered to my mom and kept apologizing to her, but the damage was done.

The sad truth is, *"Words said in anger can never be taken back."*

We need to *"Use painful events to reshape character—life is a painful teacher."*

—Unknown

Not only did I have to ask my mom for forgiveness because of what I said, but also, I had to let go of all that animosity I'd harbored against her for so many years. And offer her my forgiveness for that too.

Forgive—your life depends on it

Some people might mistake forgiveness for weakness, but the fact is it is a character strength that, when practiced, can result in a better psychological and physical health and a longer life. The individual who extends forgiveness benefits more from the act than the one forgiven.

As you saw from my experience, failing to forgive often engages thoughts of anger, vengeance, hate, and resentment that have unproductive and unhealthy outcomes.

Unforgiveness results in stress; in turn, stress causes some of the most significant health problems. In my case, it was anxiety and depression.

Other stress disorders that can be experienced include elevated blood pressure, vascular resistance, decreased immune response, asthma, obesity, diabetes, headaches, panic attacks and insomnia; it worsens gastrointestinal problems and can lead to worse outcomes in cancer and coronary artery disease, which can lead to heart attack.

You might be wondering: *How can stress make me sick? How can an emotional feeling wreak havoc on my body?*

It is important to note that stress isn't only a feeling. It isn't just in your head. It's a built-in physiologic response to a threat. When you're stressed, your body thinks you are in danger and responds. Your blood vessels constrict. Your blood pressure and pulse rise. You breathe faster. Your bloodstream is flooded with hormones such as cortisol and adrenaline.

When you're stressed all the time, those physiologic changes, over time, can lead to serious health problems.

You can reduce your stress levels by choosing to forgive and experience psychological wellbeing and a healthier life.

Oftentimes you hear of family feuds lasting for years. I even heard of one lasting over twenty years. This person is not talking to that person because of something that might have been said or done years ago.

Hanging on to grudges possibly will result in an experience of severe depression and post-traumatic stress disorder. Some people with grudges end up on medication prescribed for depression, heart disease, etc., that might have serious side effects.

If only they can forgive, their stress levels will decline, leading to improved health. And the best thing is, there are no side effects.

Speaking from experience, I can testify that forgiveness is not just about saying the words "I forgive you" but involves making a conscious decision to let go of negative feelings. It involves a release of stress, anxiety, anger, resentment, and hostility.

It does not matter if the person deserves it or not.

The following steps can help you develop a more forgiving attitude—and benefit from better emotional and physical health.

Tips on Forgiveness

1. Choose to forgive

First of all, it is important for us to understand that forgiveness is a choice. You can choose to offer compassion and grace to the person who wronged you.

2. Put your plan into action

Once you make that choice, seal it with an action. If you don't feel you can talk to the person who wronged you at that point, write about your forgiveness in a journal or even talk about it to someone you trust.

Don't let anybody fool you: to forgive is not always easy. Forgiveness for some comes effortlessly, but for most people proves to be one of the hardest things to do. It can take time to reach that point. In my experience it took months. But always bear in mind that forgiving will reap tremendous benefits for you.

3. Empathize with the other person

Try to put yourself in the other person's shoes. Sometimes this can give you a greater understanding as to why people do certain things. Not that you like or even accept the situation, but it can aid in the process of forgiving.

For instance, if your spouse grew up in a family that never said the words "I love you" to each other, you will understand why he finds it hard to say that to you.

4. Learn to forgive others' faults

Simply forgiving someone because you think you have no alternative or because you think your religion requires it may be enough to bring some healing.

However, when you forgive because you understand and accept the fact that no one is perfect, you will be able to resume a normal relationship with the other person, even if that person never apologized.

Those who only forgave in an effort to salvage the relationship wound up with a worse relationship.

5. Do not expect an apology

Sometimes pride gets in the way, preventing a person from doing the noble thing. Saying the words "I am sorry" sticks in the throat of some.

Bear in mind that an apology might not change your relationship or elicit an apology from the other. If you don't expect it, you won't be disappointed. Remember, the forgiver benefits more than the forgiven.

Growing pains

I realized that to forgive Bill and Brooke was one of my growing pains.

There are so many things in life that we can use to illustrate the existence of this process.

Gold is a highly attractive, bright, shiny, almost glowingly radiant metal that in both air and water is resistant to such depreciating factors as corrosion and rust. A very pliable and ductile metal, gold is also greatly valued for its ability to capably conduct both heat and electricity well.

Fire is a way to test gold, and when all the impurities are burned away, what's left is twenty-four-karat gold—considered very valuable indeed.

In order for gold to be refined, it must be subjected to an intense fire. This fire purifies the gold by separating out all the impurities, also known as the dross. As the dross burns away, only the pure gold remains.

It is the process of going through the fire that makes the gold pure.

Look at the difficult situations, the pain and sorrow, as the fire that helps to purify the gold—as an opportunity to grow and bring out the best in you. This is the only means by which we can grow from strength to strength.

From this you can become stronger, shine brighter, having a newfound glow that all can see. After going through my difficult moments, I had some people look at me and say, "Delia you are glowing." And no, I was not pregnant.

I know some pregnant people have a special glow, usually during their second trimester. But this glow came only from God, after going through the fire of life difficulties.

I remember when a pastor, looking at me one day, said, "God is really with you. You have this glow and look like a different person."

Some people used to say to me, "Delia, you are so strong." My humble reply was always, "My strength died a long time ago. God is my strength."

We can also see growing pains through the prism of a *butterfly*. It starts out as an egg, then becomes a caterpillar, then chrysalis, and finally turns into a butterfly.

In complete darkness, with very little space to move around, the caterpillar remains cooped up in the chrysalis. For ten to fourteen days, it appears to people on the outside seemingly dead.

However, on the inside the caterpillar's body changes, until it eventually emerges as a new creature, a beautiful butterfly.

We too go through different stages in our life cycle that can help to propel us to grow and even to reinvent ourselves.

Once I saw a picture of a caterpillar next to a cocoon, then a butterfly with the words "Give yourself time."

God is working to turn you into the best version of you.

He is molding you. Have you ever noticed how fast the pot spins on the wheel in order for the clay to be shaped, and the end result is a beautiful work of art? It can turn as fast as three hundred revolutions per minute (RPMs).

Sometimes you might feel like your life is spinning out of control. But keep holding on to your faith and never give up. These are just growing pains.

When you are going through a difficult time, think of it as a season.

The Bible speaks about seasons in Ecclesiastes 3:1–8:

To everything there is a season, and a time to every purpose under the heaven.

A time to be born, and a time to die; a time to plant, and a time to pluck up that which is planted;

A time to kill, and a time to heal; a time to break down, and a time to build up;

A time to weep, and a time to laugh; a time to mourn, and a time to dance;

A time to cast away stones, and a time to gather stones together; a time to embrace, and a time to refrain from embracing;

A time to get, and a time to lose; a time to keep, and a time to cast away;

A time to rend, and a time to sew; a time to keep silence, and a time to speak;

A time to love, and a time to hate; a time of war, and a time of peace.

Many plants are the prettiest in the autumn. Then cold, dark winter comes; the leaves now fallen off, leaves most trees looking empty and void, even lifeless, for a few months. Then comes spring, and they begin to bloom in all their glory.

A new life starts, a new beginning. So, in your difficult time, look at it as your fire, your chrysalis, the potter's wheel, or your period of winter.

Always remember, it is an opportunity for you to have a new beginning or to start a new chapter in your life.

Lessons learned

1. *You can speak things into existence so be very careful of the words you speak. Speak into life the things you wish for, only positive things. Not the things that would bring you unwanted pain and sorrow.*

2. *Take it from me: to forgive is one of the best things you can do for yourself. It may be very difficult and very rewarding at the same time. So, choose to forgive.*

3. *It is always wise to listen to and follow good advice, no matter how hard it might seem. If I had not heeded the advice of my friend to forgive Bill and Brooke, I might still be having all those negative feelings.*

CHAPTER 9

Finding Happiness Again

Don't wait for things to get easier, simpler, better.
Life will always be complicated.
Learn to be happy right now otherwise,
you will run out of time.
—Unknown

We all want to be happy. No one likes to be sad and miserable, but how do we find happiness again after going through major difficulties?

Is it even possible to be happy after your whole life falls apart—when the love of your life walks out, or you are betrayed by someone close to you?

Yes, it is!

It will not be easy because it will take some time and effort on your part to change your whole outlook on life and how to react to situations differently.

I believe that if you follow these tips, you will be able to live a fuller life and find happiness again.

1. Love yourself

Once I saw an image of a heart made by Jenny Dettrick; in it were the words *"Note to self: I Love You."*

All our time and effort go into doing things to show our husbands, children, parents, or even friends how much we love them, but what about us?

Take some time to do things to tell yourself, "I love you."

Here are some tips to help you do just that:

- **Love yourself.** For me this is quite easy because of my personality. I have always had a high self-esteem, having confidence in my worth or abilities, but for some this is one of the most demanding things to do.

    A lot of people achieve nothing in life because they do not believe in themselves. They look at themselves as worthless, a "nobody."

    Loving yourself gives you the confidence and drive to pursue and accomplish your dreams and goals.

    I want you to do a simple exercise with me right now. Write your name in the line below. Now say these words out loud:

    I love you _____

    Go even further by filling in four things you like about yourself below:

I am

1._____

2._____

3._____

4._____

Now say them aloud.

By saying these words to yourself every day, you will change your attitude and thoughts about yourself in a positive way.

- **Take time for you.** This is a very important part of loving yourself. As women, we get so caught up in life—taking care of our husbands, kids, parents; doing chores; or even studying and working to pursue our careers—that we neglect to save time for ourselves.

  As important as those other things are, you need to do things that make you happy. Buy a nice dress, go to the spa, get a pedicure, manicure, even a massage. Live your life to the fullest.

  Doing these activities with a girlfriend is even more fun. Remember that you are good enough, and you are worth it.

  You don't even have to leave the house or spend a lot of money.

  You can take some "me" time by reading a nice book, luxuriating in a soaking bath, or both, or watching a movie, knitting, painting, etc. Whatever helps to soothe you and makes you happy. One of my happiest "me" times is taking a bath while listening to my favorite songs. It relaxes me.

Another one I enjoy is some "shopping therapy." Even if I don't have much money to spend, I find going around into the shops, looking at dresses, shoes, and bags and finding great bargains very therapeutic for me. This is what I run to many times to help me when I am feeling very overwhelmed.

I have known of a person who took up gardening as a coping mechanism. Whenever she finds it hard to deal with a situation, she takes a time-out in the garden. Just being around the plants or flowers, watering and taking care of them, and she feels peace and calmness like in the eye during a hurricane. If you haven't already found your coping mechanism, I implore you to go out there and try new things until you do.

- **Loving yourself helps you love others deeper.** Many of us fall into the unhealthy habit of looking at ourselves and finding all sorts of things we don't like. We tend to be our worst critic. Maybe you don't like the shape of your nose, eyes, toes, etc. This can negatively affect your self-esteem. It can be very hard to truly love someone else if you do not even love yourself. When you love yourself, this can result in a more fulfilling and rewarding relationship with others.

- **Loving yourself means that you will not allow others to mistreat and abuse you.** How you love yourself is how you teach others to love you. Remember the golden rule? *"Do unto others as you would have them do unto you"* (Matthew 7:12). If people around you see that you are constantly doing things to hurt yourself and have no regard to what happens to you, they might begin to treat you the same way. Why wouldn't they follow your example? However, by loving, respecting, and valuing yourself, you are setting the bar for how others should treat you.

2. Accept the things you cannot change

The Serenity Prayer by the theologian Reinhold Niebuhr goes like this:

> God grant me the serenity to accept
> the things I cannot change,
> Courage to change the things I can,
> and Wisdom to know the difference.

If we adhere to these words full of great wisdom, it can save us a lot of heartache and pain.

- *Accept* the fact that you cannot control the actions of other people, only yourself. A lot of times people break promises; people betray us. The impact is a lot greater if they are people we love.

The sad thing is, this is a part of life.

In my situation Bill and Brooke promised to keep their relationship professional but didn't.

What do we do in such a case?

Many people get frustrated and angry and end up doing things that they later regret.

I had to reach the point of accepting that no matter how hard I tried or what I did, I could in no way control Bill or Brooke's behaviour.

God created us all free agents. Some of us might wish we had a remote control to use on others, to command their behaviour. But only in science fiction and in movies like *Click* does that exist.

The sooner we accept this fact, the better.

- *Accept* the fact that not everyone will even like you. Some people, knowing nothing about you—seeing you for the very first time—might decide they don't. Most times, they do not come out and say the words" I don't like you." However, their actions reflect this.

So, what do you do?

Should you do everything to get the person to like you, including changing yourself?

It is never pleasant to hear negative things about yourself.

What do I do? If I know it is not true, as soon as those negative remarks go through one ear, I let them go straight out through the other. I do not dwell on them.

I suggest you do the same.

- *Accept* that we cannot change the future. There is nobody on earth who can truly predict the future. Not the astrologist, psychic, magician or meteorologist. They might make an educated guess and many times are wrong in their predictions.

  How many times has the meteorologist predicted sunshine, and then rain poured cats and dogs?

  Stop worrying about what will happen tomorrow. Worry never changes anything. As a matter of fact, most of the time it makes things worse because we end up with headaches, ulcers, anxiety, depression, even heart attacks, and the list goes on.

- *Accept* the fact that you cannot please everyone. This is a lesson I learned very early in life. So many times, we try to be and do everything to everybody. I can tell you now: this is an impossible task.

- *Accept* your past mistakes. All of us have made a number of mistakes at some point. However, beating ourselves up and constantly dwelling on our mistakes is unhealthy and prevents us from moving on with our lives. I do believe that we should evaluate our mistakes and learn from them so we can try to avoid repeating them.

We cannot change what has already happened, but we can change what we do now and in the future.

I remember one of my counselors sending me this poem:

Yesterday, Today and Tomorrow

There are two days in every week about which we should not worry,

two days which should be kept free from fear and apprehension.

One of these is yesterday with its mistakes and cares, its faults and blunders, its aches and pains.

All the money in the world cannot bring back yesterday.

Yesterday has passed forever beyond our control.

We cannot undo a single act we performed.

We cannot erase a single word we said.

Yesterday is gone.

The other day we should not be worried about is tomorrow with its possible adversities, its burdens, its large promise or poor performance. Tomorrow is also beyond our immediate control.

Tomorrow's sun will rise either in splendour or behind a mask of clouds—but it will rise.

And until it does we have no stake in tomorrow, for it is yet unborn.

That leaves only one day . . . Today.

Any man can fight the battles of just one day,

it is only when you and I add the burdens of those two awful eternities, Yesterday and Tomorrow that we break down.

It isn't the experience of today that drives us mad, it is the remorse or bitterness which happened and the dread of what tomorrow may bring.
Let us therefore, live one day at a time.
Always bear in mind that "nothing is permanent."
Don't stress yourself too much,
because no matter how bad the situation is it will change!
Keep holding on, keep fighting, and never give up on life.

—Eva Boros-Furesz

3. Focus on the people who care about you

Don't let the people who aren't worth it get you down. Focus on those who love and accept you for who you are and shower them with love.

—Unknown

When going through difficult times, a lot of people tend to push away those who love and care for them. The pain is so severe that they are upset with the whole world. But these are the moments when we need the support and love of those we love even more. It can help you tremendously.

In my case, I started to focus on my sons and being there for them, which helped me a great deal.

Another thing to do is to accept the hand held out by family and friends. Allow them to bear the burden with you. I accepted my friend Onel's offer to help me with the kids and my chores. It was very beneficial not just to me but to my kids as well.

4. Get involved

When you do nothing, you feel overwhelmed and powerless. But when you get involved, you feel the sense of hope and accomplishment that comes from knowing you are working to make things better.

—Maya Angelou

Find something you are passionate about. Participate in activities you love, or be brave enough to try new things. The aim is to do something you enjoy doing.

Helping others is one way you can get involved. Sometimes we get so engulfed in our own problems we fail to see the many people suffering around us, some of whom are going through much worse situations than we are.

Consciously open your eyes and heart to those around you.

I love to help people in whatever way I can. I had always wanted to assist in feeding the homeless, so it's one of the things I started to do.

Helping others is not only good for them but also helps make us happier and healthier too.

This will:

- take your focus off your problems and lessen the time spent worrying—giving you a well-needed break.
- take you out of the house, which sometimes is one of the hardest things for someone during difficult, depressing times.

5. *Choose your inner circle wisely*

Surround yourself with positive people and you'll be a positive person.

—Kellie Pickler

Whenever you are going through a difficult time, it is critical that you know (1) whom to listen to and (2) whom to have in your inner circle.

This is quite evident in the story of Job in the Bible: Job 2, when his friends Eliphaz, Bildad, and Zophar visited him. Bilad called him a liar and accused him of sinning; that, he said, was why all these terrible things were befalling him.

Instead of encouraging and helping Job, his so-called friends went as far as to call him a hypocrite. Surely this was not helpful to Job but just added more misery to his suffering. They made an appointment to come to mourn with him and comfort him, but they had done the opposite.

Depending on what you are going through, a lot of people have a lot to say—giving advice and their opinion on the matter.

However, some people, in an effort to try and help, will put you down by the words they say or things they do rather than build you up. Sometimes even those you love.

If they are always doing this, you might need to step away from those people towards those who bring comfort and care.

Onel, even though she did not say much, just being there and helping me every way she could, made a significant difference. Do you know the seventeenth-century poet/cleric John Donne's quotation from his *Devotions for Emergent Occasions*, "No man is an island"?

We all need somebody sometime.

6. *Have the right mindset*

A positive attitude gives you power over your circumstances instead of your circumstances having power over you.

—*Joyce Meyer*

Having the right mindset can make a tremendous difference in your life. How can I cultivate the right mindset? Here are a few tips:

- **You are responsible for your own happiness.** First of all, come to the realization—and bear in mind—that you are responsible for your own happiness. It must come from within not from outside sources such as material things or your partner, kids, etc.

   Don't think for a moment that your husband's or boyfriend's job is to make you happy or that having a bigger house or a more expensive car will make you happy. It is true that these sometimes bring a sense of happiness. But what happens if they are taken away?

   Will you still be happy, or will your whole life fall apart? You don't need to have a husband or partner or kids to be happy. Find happiness despite who or what is around you.

- **Have a positive attitude.** It means that you believe in yourself by maintaining the "yes, I can" attitude. If we do not have confidence in ourselves, we can be our biggest roadblock on our path to achieve greatness. I think the first step to achieving your goals is to believe in yourself.

- **Know that you are loved.** Even if no one in this world loves you, you know that God loves you. The famous Bible text John 3:16 tells us, "For God so loved the world that he gave his one and only Son, that whoever believes in him shall not perish but have eternal life." Knowing and believing that God will always love me brought great comfort to me.

- **Be careful what you watch, read, and listen to.** These can influence your mindset. For instance, if you are suffering from a broken heart, don't waddle in your sadness by listening to sad love songs. Try not to listen to songs that are sad and depressing like "I Have Nothing" ("I have nothing, nothing, nothing if I don't have you") by Whitney Houston or "Without You" ("I can't live if living is without you") by Mariah Carey.

  Instead, listen to positive songs, like "Still I Rise" or "This Too Shall Pass" both by Yolanda Adams, "Smile" by Kirk Franklin, "I Will Survive" by Gloria Gaynor, "Don't Worry Be Happy" by Bobby Mc Ferrin, or "Happy" by Pharrell Williams. One of my favorites was "God Favored Me" by Hezekiah Walker.

These are some of the songs I listened to when I was going through my problems. And watch encouraging films that will inspire you.

Can you think of what the world would be like without music? Singing brings joy to the heart. While growing up, I kept hearing on the radio, "If there was no music, I would have died a long time ago." Music soothes the soul and can bring happiness to our hearts if even for but a moment. *A beautiful day begins with a beautiful mindset. Don't let your circumstances make you think that you cannot create a new reality for yourself. When you wake up, take a second to think about what a privilege it is to simply be alive. Take a moment to look at all the things that are going right in your life. Whenever we are facing a difficult situation in our lives we seem to only focus on that. The moment we start acting like life is a blessing I assure you it will start to feel like one.*

—*John Geiger*

7. *Protect your psyche*

Anything that costs you your peace is too expensive.

—*Unknown*

Make a conscious decision to protect your psyche and take the necessary steps to follow through.

Leave everything and everyone in your life that constantly has a negative impact on your mental wellbeing. Doing this can prevent you from having a nervous breakdown. If someone or a certain situation is detrimental to your mental health, the best thing to do is to remove yourself.

I decided to leave the matrimonial home. In your situation you might find it necessary to leave something else.

For instance, a teenager might have to decide to close their social media accounts due to online bullying, etc.

Mental health is one of the most talked-about topics today, especially after going through the Covid-19 pandemic.

8. Be contented in life

Happiness is not about getting all you want; it is about enjoying all you have.

—Unknown

Being content with what you have can give you peace of mind. A lot of people are so miserable and unhappy in life because they want what they don't or can't have. They want what the "Joneses" have: a bigger car, a bigger house, more expensive clothes and shoes, etc. You will save yourself a lot of heartache and pain if you focus on the things, you have and adopt a grateful attitude.

I have always been content with what I have, never looking at what others have and yearned for it. My philosophy has been, *"What is mine is mine."*

So, I encourage you to do the same. Don't compare yourself to the Joneses and what they have but find happiness with what you have.

9. *Know when to let go*

Some people believe holding on and hanging in there are signs of great strength. However, there are times when it takes much more strength to know when to let go and then do it.

—*Ann Landers*

Knowing when to let go of bad situations can save you a lot of heartache and pain in life and even save your life.

As hard as it might be to accept, some people are meant to be in your life for but a season. A lot of women hold onto toxic relationships in fear. Fear of being alone. Or they are fearful they might let someone down—their family and friends—if they leave.

Some hold on because they feel they love the person so much and do not have the strength to leave. Others because they don't believe in divorce and would rather stay and suffer.

Still others—not working—are financially dependent; fear they could not provide for themselves and their children if they were to leave.

Like in my case, one of the questions that will go through a person's mind after being cheated on is, *"Do I stay or leave?"*

Here is a case in point—about a woman I will call Dolores.

She knew her husband was cheating but decided to stay in that relationship for fifteen years. She held everything inside; all the hurt and pain, she bore on her own. However, she continued to carry out her wifely duties—cooking, ironing, etc.—for him, maybe hoping and thinking he would change one day. Spoiler alert: in the end, he left her to move in with his mistress.

Sadly, Dolores later died of cancer, most likely worsened by the many years of unhappiness and stress.

We often hear that stress is the number-one killer in the world and the root of many illnesses we face in life. That's why it's so important to know when to let go and also talk to someone you trust. Someone you know has your best interests at heart, someone you can confide in. The longer you stay and hold all those emotions of pain and hurt inside, the more detrimentally it can affect your health.

Letting go can actually save your life.

10. Take your burdens to Jesus

"God doesn't want us to carry our burdens. He asks us to lay them down at the foot of the cross. He wants us to surrender our heavy loads to him."

—*Country Thang Daily*

Lay down your burdens. Don't pick them back up. Give them all to Jesus. In Matthew 11:28, He says, "Come unto me, all ye that labour and are heavy laden, and I will give you rest."

He promises to always be there and never leave us. There is no way I would be able to make it through my difficulties if I did not have God in my life.

Just the thought of knowing there is someone I can talk to any time of the day or night—it cost me nothing. I have a direct line to Him through prayer—this is so comforting to me: having someone to tell all my troubles to, to confide in and know that He will not spread it to others. Sharing everything that causes me pain and sorrow. Not just that but also my happy moments as well.

The only one who knows the beginning and the end.

I find peace when I go before Him, the way a child feels in the presence of a loving parent.

I don't know what I would do if He weren't in my life. In fact, many times I wonder, how do people make it in life without God?

I can tell you one thing: I would not be here today if it weren't for God, who is my source of help and strength.

There is a lot of talk today about faith, but what is more important is putting our faith into action. Lay your burden down at the feet of Jesus and trust that He will take care of you. I have learnt that this is one of the most important steps you can take on your journey to become happy again.

No matter what I go through in life, I know that I am never alone. God is always with me to sustain and comfort me.

I must say that for me *God is the only source of true happiness*. You can follow all the tips above and still feel like something is lacking. God is like the glue that sticks everything together.

The reason I decided to write this book is to empower women who have faced infidelity, betrayal, or loss to find happiness again and live a full life. To know that this is not the end, but it can be the beginning of a new chapter in their life.

I have been able to fight my way through my difficult moments and find happiness again.

How did I do that? I have already shared with you many things I have done over the years. Some of which are accepting what I cannot change, allowing myself to go through the grief process, forgiving those who have wronged me, looking forward in life, trying new things, taking steps to take care of me, and choosing to be happy.

Make one of the best decisions you can make in life and choose to be happy. You Can Be Happy Again!

Lessons Learned

1. *Make sure, no matter what you might be going through, to take care of you. Only then will you be able to take care of others. "Taking good care of yourself helps you to take good care of others."*

2. *You can use your mess to bless. I am a firm believer that sometimes God allows us to go through certain situations in life to put us in a better position to help someone else going through a similar situation. So, take any*

opportunity you get to give advice and help where possible. Look at how you can use your experience to help someone else.

3. *It is very important to focus on the future and not on the past, a lesson that had a big impact on my life and helped me to cope.*

4. *Knowing when to let go has proven crucial in coping with my situation. I do not know where I'd be today if I had not let go.*

Epilogue

Will I ever find love again? Will I ever be able to give my heart to another man? These questions plagued my mind often.

After my experience with Bill, I just figured all men were the same and vowed to stay away from them. I was very content and happy with just living with my kids. Shunning men, I kept a distance from them, trying by all means to protect myself and my heart. As far as I was concerned, they were all liars and no good.

Yet, on occasions, during those lonely moments when I yearned for companionship and love—when I saw couples seemingly so in love—I longed to find my knight in shining armor. It was only human to miss and yearn for what I had before.

There was a battle raging inside me—a tug of war where at one point side A seemed to be winning and another time Side B. It went on like that for almost three years.

Until I met Osman.

He spoke all the right words and did all the right things to make me feel special and loved.

Being very attracted to him, I fell deep into the love zone.

I told him about the pain and hurt I suffered from my last relationship with Bill, and he assured me he would never treat me that way.

You know what? I believed him.

Thoughts and fears of being hurt again went out the window.

This was true love. Once again. I had been lucky enough to find it twice.

Everything seemed to be going great, or so I thought.

Never did I imagine I was about to face yet another major challenge, the kind I had not experienced with Bill.

This time I was to suffer from psychological and emotional abuse along with coercive control tactics. It brought me to the brink of a nervous breakdown. I started having throbbing headaches every day and reached the point where I literally felt like there was electricity flowing through my brain.

At the first sign that the abuse was going to get physical, I left the abusive relationship with my two-year-old child, who was with me at the time, less than £10 and not knowing where I was going.

Find out more in my next book.

ACKNOWLEDGMENTS

I have a deep debt of gratitude to my wonderful children. Thank you for your support; for accepting when I could not cook a hot meal or take you out and spend the time I should have with you because I was busy writing. You are my greatest treasure, and I love you all so much.

To my mentor and former coach, Dr. Nadine Collins, thank you for starting me on my journey to becoming an author. I will forever be grateful.

A special thank you to Margaret Harrell, my editor, who went above and beyond her call of duty; so kind, patient, and very resourceful, freely giving advice and willing to help in every way she can.

Also, to all my family and friends who encouraged me along the way, thank you.

Finally, to you the readers of my book, *You Can Be Happy Again: Bouncing Back After Infidelity, Betrayal, and Loss,* a heartfelt thank-you for choosing this book. My hope and prayer is that it will help you to find the happiness you deserve.

ABOUT THE AUTHOR

Delia Gould is originally from the beautiful island of St. Vincent and the Grenadines in the Caribbean but now resides in the United Kingdom. She is a dedicated Christian, who loves the Lord, and is also the proud mother of three wonderful children.

Delia is a qualified Chartered Certified Accountant, with over twenty years' experience in this field. Her first job was at Pannell Kerr Forster.

She is a firm believer that sometimes God allows us to go through experiences solely to better position us to help other people in similar situations. She hopes that this book, in which she shares her experiences, will have a positive and life-changing impact on those who read it.

Did you enjoy reading this book?

Then I would appreciate your leaving a review on Amazon and my book landing page: <u>deliagould.com</u>. You can also email me here: youcanbehappyagain2@gmail.com.

Speaker Mentorship platform

Are you facing difficulties in life and struggling to find happiness again, or do you know of someone who is?

I am the creator of the You Can Be Happy Again Model™ that helps women between the ages of thirty and sixty-five who have faced infidelity, betrayal, and loss of any kind, to heal, grow, and choose to be happy again.

I created this model, having realized that many women are suffering in silence; they need support and practical advice to get them through these difficult times.

Get in contact with me. I will be happy to partner with you, your church, or other organization to help more women learn how to reclaim their happiness.

Printed by Amazon Italia Logistica S.r.l.
Torrazza Piemonte (TO), Italy

54585988R10150